1.00

FINANCIAL RELATIONS OF GREECE AND THE GREAT POWERS, 1832-1862

JON V. KOFAS

EAST EUROPEAN MONOGRAPHS, BOULDER
DISTRIBUTED BY COLUMBIA UNIVERSITY PRESS
NEW YORK

1981

for

Peter A. Pappas
and
Jim Kofas

TABLE OF CONTENTS

INTRODUCTION

One of the most unfortunate aspects of Modern Greek history is the continued foreign intervention which that nation has suffered since her independence. One of the reasons which caused European intervention in Greek domestic affairs during the nineteenth century was due to Greece's overdependence on the Great Powers for financial aid.

Foreign borrowing started in Greece during the War of Independence under the most strenuous conditions. The provisional government during the Revolution was optimistic about European enthusiasm and willingness to embrace the Greek struggle for independence. The insurgent Greek leaders did not realize the devastating consequences that foreign loans could have if the nation defaulted. Foreign loans were given diplomatic significance and were generally regarded with a high degree of enthusiasm as though they were gifts.

The Greeks entertained such illusions concerning foreign borrowing partly because the events of the Revolution overwhelmed them to the degree that they could not forsee the long term negative effects of foreign loans. In 1824 and 1825 the revolutionary government contracted large loans from Great Britain and the trend of foreign borrowing continued until 1836. As a small and economically weak nation, however, Greece defaulted after 1843 and lost her credit standing in the European community. As a result of her default to the Great Powers who had guaranteed Greece a 60,000,000 francs loan in 1832, the Protectorate suffered continuous foreign intervention in her domestic, political and economic affairs.

From the establishment of the Greek kingdom in 1832 until the 1862 revolution which ended King Otho's reign, the Powers violated the sovereignty of Greece on numerous occasions. Great Britain was the protagonist Power in violating Greek independence as a result of her determination to dominate Greek politics. The justification which the Foreign Office used for Britain's interventionist policy in Greece was the latter's default on her foreign debt. In 1850 Palmerston ordered the Pireaus port blockaded using as an excuse the default of the Greek foreign debt. From May 1854 to February 1857 Great Britain and France occupied Greece because the latter sided with Russia in the Crimean War. The Western Powers did not lift the occupation until Greece and her ally, Russia, agreed to the establishment of a Financial Commission whose purpose was to examine the Protectorate's finances and introduce solutions to the Greek authorities concerning the liquidation of the country's foreign debt.

The Financial Commission's investigations persisted for more than two years and were a blatant violation of the Treaty of 1832, which guaranteed Greece her independence. Finally, in 1862 when anti-monarchists revolts broke out at Nauplion the Powers assisted the revolutionaries' cause by not extending any financial aid to the King and preventing him from engaging in domestic borrowing. The Powers financial relations with Greece from the War of Independence until Otho's exile in 1862 are closely examined in this study to determine the effect of foreign loans in diplomatic relations.

CHAPTER I

GREEK FOREIGN BORROWING DURING THE REVOLUTION

A. *The Loan of 1824*

The Greek War of Independence which the *Philike Etairia* (Friendly Society) sparked from Odessa in 1821 was a long struggle of nearly a decade and it required material and human sacrifices to guarantee its success.[1] The national consciousness of the Greeks was sufficiently strong to endure the necessary sacrifices in order to achieve national autonomy. The Greek people under the Ottoman yoke lacked, however, the material resources to carry out the revolution against the Turks successfully. One of the factors which contributed to the financially weak insurgent Greece was the poorly organized central government. From 1821 until 1827 there were constant power struggles between the various Greek factions which assumed leadership roles in the Revolution.[2]

The provisional government's weakness and lack of national support left leadership responsibilities and elaborate administrative tasks upon the hands of local "Captains" and Chieftains.[3] The people trusted their local leaders more than they did an unknown group of men who had proclaimed themselves as the provisional government. The local leaders organized the people to fight and imposed upon them their military as well as civilian authority by tax collection to finance the War.[4]

There are no exact figures indicating the amount of the contribution to the Greek struggle, but some evidence does exist. The provisional government raised a domestic loan of 500,000 grosia (21.50 pounds sterling = 100 grosia). The government also confiscated the churches' and monasteries' gold and silver which amounted to 140,000 grosia.[5]

Many of the contributions which financed the War, however, originated in Europe. Wealthy Greeks throughout Europe and the Near East as well as European philhellenes contributed generously to the revolution.[6] There is no possible method of determining the exact amount of the philhellenes' contributions' but Professor A. M. Andreades calculated that during the first six years of the Revolution the Greek expenditure was 70,116,828 grosia,[7] a substantial portion of which originated from voluntary contributions by European philhellenes and Greeks of the diaspora.[8]

One of the most important sources which financed the Greek Revolution however was the National property.[9] The State property was originally Turkish property in Greece, but during the War of Independence it fell into the hands of the Greek provisional government.[10] The largest portions of the National Estates were productive farms which the government leased in order to raise State revenues.[11] The provisional government, however, did not utilize the National property to its fullest potential in order to yield maximum revenue for insurgent Greece.

According to the statistical report which President John Kapodistrias[12] compiled for the Great Powers from 1828 to 1831, Greece claimed 47,516 square kilometers of land, of which 4,320,960 *stremmata* belonged to the State.[13] Three million of the total National Domain was in Peloponnesos but as the chart below indicates most of the public revenues came from the islands. This was proof therefore of the Greek government's insufficient use of the State property.

Crete	7,383,620 grosia
Islands	1,419,100 grosia
Peloponnese	2,605,800 grosia
Eastern Greece	729,500 grosia
Western Greece	708,200 grosia
Total	12,846,220 grosia[14]

The above figures represent the total revenues of 1823 and 1824. The expenditure for 1823, however, was 38,616,000 grosia.[15] The enormous deficit was due to the cost of maintaining a substantial military force,[16] but the provisional government could have reduced that astonishing deficit if it distributed and sold large portions of the National property.

The government did not adopt such measures for it .held the National Domain as a public trust[17] because it realized that the land could be mortgaged to European financiers when the need arose to contract foreign loans.[18] Many revolutionary leaders (the chieftains primarily) urged the National Assembly to reward plots of land to the thousands who fought against the Turks.[19] The government of.icials, however, did not yield to those demands for they considered such a resolution unrealistic since they believed that the National Estates were the sole financial foundation for insurgent Greece.[20]

In view of the exuberant 1823 deficit of the Public Treasury Greek officials sent a delegation to Europe in order to raise a loan. The idea of raising a loan from the European community appealed to the provisional government not only because the Europeans could aid Greece financially but with the financial aid the government hoped to gain E·1rope's moral and diplomatic support. The politicians of Insurgent Greece drew that conclusion concerning the political implications of European financial aid because they realized that in the post-Napoleonic era of Metternician conservatism, Greece would indeed score a great victory if it secured a European loan. Prince Metternich, chancellor of Austria, and Viscount Castlereagh, British foreign secretary, wished to retain the *status quo* in the Balkans and the two statesmen feldt that the Greek War of Independence was an obstacle to the European balance of power.[21] Their opposition to the Greek struggle eliminated the provisional government's hopes of contracting a loan with the European Powers.

Since the European governments had not embraced the Greek struggle, the provisional government hoped to obtain a loan from philhellenes who had shown their whole-hearted support of Greece since the outbreak of the Revolution. The European philhellenic movements started at the beginning of the nineteenth century primarily by intellectuals who admired, idealized and sympathized with the Greek people.[22] There were several reasons behind the Europeans' embracement of the Greek cause. The most important of these reasons were religious, intellectual and economic. The Christian Europeans championed the cause of the Greek Orthodox population which struggled to free itself from Moslem captivity. Intellectuals admired the ancient Greeks for their contribution to Western civilization and wished to see the modern Greeks free. And

finally the European business community favored Greek independence
because of the close association between Greek merchants and European
entrepreneurs during the early nineteenth century. The provisional government exploited European favoratism toward Greece and attempted to use
it in order to further its cause of defeating the Ottoman Empire and
reestablishing the lost Byzantine empire.

Greek attempts to raise foreign loans started in 1821 but with minimal
success. In November 1821 the Greek government secured 102,000
florins from wealthy Greek merchants in Europe.[23] In March 1822 the
National Assembly authorized a delegation to borrow one million Spanish
dollars, placing the National Estates as mortgage for the loan.[24] The
National Assembly selected Andreas Louriotes to represent Greece in
Europe and authorized him to negotiate the loan. In 1823 Louriotes
went to Italy and Germany in search of financiers but his attempts failed
so he proceeded to his next destination, Spain.[25] The Greek envoy was
not any more successful in Spain than he was in Italy and Germany
because Spain suffered consecutive deficits from 1820 until 1823 and
relied on large foreign loans to pay her debts.[26] While in Spain Louriotes
met Edward Blaquiere, a British captain, who sympathized with the
Greeks in their efforts to achieve national autonomy. Blaquiere persuaded
the Greek envoy to leave Spain and to go London where the possibilities
of securing a loan there were greater than in any other European city.[27]
Louriotes and Blaquiere went to England where the British sea captain
introduced the Greek delegate to several philhellenes of notable political
and financial status.[28] Blaquiere helped to organize the prestigeous London Greek Committee whose membership included thirty-one politicians
in Parliament, a number of wealthy financiers, officers of the British
military and other philhellene enthusiasts.[29]

The Committee's secretary was Sir John Bowring, a British entrepreneur. Originally there were thirty-one members who belonged to
the London Greek Committee, but membership quickly increased to
eighty-seven.[30] After Blaquiere succeeded in establishing the Committee
in London he went to Greece where he persuaded the provisional government to authorize the raising of a loan in London. The revolutionary
government, headed by Alexander Mavrokordatos since January 1822,[31]
welcomed Blaquiere's proposal with enthusiasm and optimism.[32] The
members of the government[33] were pro-Western and especially pro-British

so they readily accepted Blaquiere's proposal. The pro-Russian chieftains headed by Theodore Kolokotrones,[34] however, "probably looked upon Blaquiere as an agent of the British government..." and opposed his proposals.[35] Other European philhellenes offered to lend money to Greece before Blaquiere's proposal[36] but the Greek government declined the offers. Mavrokordatos decided that it was in the best national interests to raise the loan in London so that Greece could gain the favor of British foreign policy.

The provisional government appointed John Orlandos, Andrew Louriotes and John Zaimes as the delegates in charge of negotiating the loan.[37] Mavrokordatos and his government asked the delegates to negotiate the loan based upon the following terms: (A) The loan should be contracted on standard currency, and the price of issue should be sixty percent; (B) the terms of payment should be set for ten to twenty years; (C) the interest, from six percent to eight percent; and (D) guarantee for the loan was the National property.[38] These were terms which the provisional government hoped to achieve but the Greeks were hardly in a favorable bargaining position. The country's future in 1823 was uncertain at best and everyone including the profit-minded European financiers knew that the fate of Greece rested with European intervention in favor of Greece and on the Ottoman empire's continuing weakness.

Blaquiere returned to London and attempted to convince the skeptics in that city's business community that Greece was a nation worth the investment. The Captain's speech below to the London Committee is an indication of his sympathy and fascination with the struggling Greeks.

> I should have no hesitation whatever in estimating the physical strength of regenerated Greece to be fully equal to that of the whole South American continent... the prospect of wealth and prosperity is almost boundless.[39]

This was obviously not one of Blaquiere's sober moments, but there was a certain element of truth in his speech. At the end of the eighteenth century and the beginning of the nineteenth Greek entrepreneurs throughout Europe made enormous fortunes and became known to businessmen as well as politicians.[40] The Greek shipping industry played a great role in propagandizing Hellenic independence in Europe. And since the provisional government rested in the hands of wealthy shipowners the Europeans trusted them[41] more than they trusted Greek captains and chieftains of unknown reputation who led at the local level. Lazarus and George Koundouriotes as well as Orlandos, the Greek delegate in London, were wealthy shipowners with notable reputations who enjoyed the trust of British politicians and entrepreneurs.

Louriotes and Orlandos arrived in London on 14 January 1824, in a congenial atmosphere which Blaquiere and the philhellenic Committee prepared for them. It would indeed be naive to assume that the British financiers were willing to negotiate a loan for Greece simply because they trusted the wealthy shipowners in charge of the country's government, or because the philhellenic Committee in London was determined to aid Greece. Admitedly these were contributing factors to the financiers' readiness to raise a loan for the deprived nation. The primary motive, however, behind such an eager group of bankers who wished to lend money to Greece was profit. From 1818 to 1824 London bankers advanced up to 47,815,000 pounds sterling in loans to European and Latin American countries.[42] Great Britain experienced an economic boom in 1823 and the "speculative era" of the early 1820s, as one historian has labeled it, was advantageous to the Greeks who were in the market for a loan.[43] London bankers were anxious to find borrowers who wished to contract loans at high interest rates. The reason for this was that the great availability of money circulation in that city caused the interest notes to drop and this was precisely why British financiers loaned money to small and weak nations in Latin America and Europe.[44]

In spite of the favorable London money-market, the Greek envoys met with some opposition in England from the Levant Company merchants who traded primarily with the Ottoman empire. The Levant merchants opposed the Greek War of Independence because it interfered with their commercial interests in the Near East.[45] The Levant Company tried vigorously to prevent London bankers from issuing a loan to Greece when Orlandos and Louriotes arrived in that city in 1824.[46] The Greek cause, however, was popular in most sectors of the London business community and the British financiers were more anxious in promoting their own interest than they were in serving those of the Levant Company. The Levant merchants therefore failed in their efforts to block Louriotes' and Orlandos' loan plans.

The Greek delegates arrived in London without any knowledge of British Banking Houses and they were caught in a disadvantageous position for they had to rely on the London Greek Committee's advice on this matter. The delegates discussed with the Committee the options before them but did not arrive at any conclusions. John Bowring, the Committee's secretary, sought the opportunity to profit from the delegation's ignorance. Without notifying anyone in the Committee, including the Greek envoys, he contracted the Greek loan with the Banking House of Loughman, O'Brien, Ellice and Company. The bank promised Bowring 10,000 to 11,000 pounds sterling if he persuaded the Greek envoys to take their business to Loughman, O'Brien, Ellice and Company. The London Committee's Secretary sacrificed his devotion to the Greek struggle in return for cash and delivered Louriotes and Orlandos to the Loughman and Company Bank.[47]

When the envoys learned that Bowring concluded an agreement for the Greek loan with a bank of his choice without notifying them or the Committee, they expressed their discontent with the Secretary's decision which they believed was contrary to the best interests of Greece.[48] The bank and the Secretary of the London Greek Committee set the price of issue for the loan at fifty-nine percent not sixty percent which Orlandos and Louriotes wanted, and according to one of the articles on the contract, Greece was held responsible for the fifty-nine percent issue price even in case of bankruptcy.[49] Furthermore, Bowring's arrangement with the bank entitled British commissioners, Lord Byron, Thomas Gordon and Leister Stanhope, all devoted philhellenes, to be in charge of the remitted loan funds.[50] The bank did not appoint a Greek delegation in charge of the funds because of fear that it would turn funds over to one of the Greek factions and the loan would not be applied towards its intended destination.

Orlandos and Louriotes convinced the philhellenes to accept at least one Greek commissioner among the three British. Lazaros Koundouriotes, who was a member of the Koundouriotes faction enjoyed the privilege of becoming the fourth delegate.[51] The Koundouriotes faction therefore had control over the loan from the time it was contracted. After this matter was resolved there were still more issues of disagreement between the British financiers and the Greek delegation. The British bank which issued the loan wanted to make a maximum profit from the vulnerable

Greeks and decided not to issue it in pounds sterling but in Spanish currency (distela). If the bank had its wish Greece would have suffered a four to five percent loss because of the devaluation price of the distela in the London currency markets.[52] The bank finally compromised with the Greek envoys and issued seventy-five percent of the loan in British pounds sterling and twenty-five percent in Spanish currency.[53] The last disagreement between the Greeks and the Loughman, O'Brien and Ellice Bank was over the issue of where the funds should be deposited. The Greek envoys wanted a Greek bank in Zante to handle the funds transaction whereas the British financiers wanted the money to be deposited in a British-owned bank in Zante. The interested parties finally agreed that both the Greek-owned and British-owned banks in Zante would be in charge of the loan funds.

On 24 February 1824, the envoys and the bank signed the loan contract in London for the nominal sum of 800,000 sterling pounds. The price of issue was fifty-nine percent which meant that buyers of bonds which were worth 100 sterling pounds only paid 59 sterling pounds. They were not required to pay the entire sum, however, but only 10 sterling pounds on each bond with the rest of the instalments spread over a period of several months.[54] The price of issue amounted to 454,700 sterling pounds after the bank deducted its fees for service on the loan. The rate of interest was five percent and the annual instalment payment interest was one percent a total of six percent amounting to 48,000 sterling pounds annually. The table on the following page indicates the extractions from the loan for various charges and expenses. After all the deductions from the principal of 800,000 sterling pounds, the sum left for Greece was 298,700 sterling pounds.

The Hellenic government pledged as a guarantee for payment to the bondholders, the National Estates, the custom duties, the salt mines and the fisheries. As a guarantee for payment on the interest the government pledged the public revenues and as an ultimate payment for the principal all the National Estates.[56]

The terms of the first foreign loan were very severe and not exactly what the provisional government wanted to achieve. All things considered, however, the Greek authorities regarded the first loan as their first financial and political victory in Europe. The Hydriot-based government of Phanariotes[57] and shipowners also regarded the loan as a decisive

Extractions from the 1824 Loan[55]

Downpayment for two years interest. . . . . . 80,000 pounds sterling
Instalment charges for two years . . . . 16,000 pounds sterling
Military supplies and ammunition. . . . . . . 9,900 pounds sterling
Relief for Messolongi . . . . 2,400 pounds sterling
Delegation expenses for one year . . . . 5,000 pounds sterling
Orlandos' personal expenses . . . . 5,900 pounds sterling
Repayment to Lord Byron for his loan
    to Greece. . . . . 4,000 pounds sterling
Extraordinary expenses . . . . 5,300 pounds sterling
Expenses for the 1825 Loan . . . . 27,500 pounds sterling
TOTAL. . . . . 156,000 pounds sterling

diplomatic victory.[58] This was obviously an illusion on their part for the Foreign Office had nothing to do with the British bank which contracted the loan. Koundouriotes, Mavrokordatos, Orlandos and other Greek officials failed to realize at the time that British bankers did not always lend money to countries with which Great Britain had favorable diplomatic relations.[59] Furthermore, the Greeks never stopped to consider that the banks in England prefered to make loans to small nations as they did so from 1822 to 1824, at high interest rates.[60]

Historians of Modern Greek studies acknowledge the unfavorable terms of the loan and the effects, both financial and political which that loan had throughout the nineteenth century. There are two schools of thought, however, on the question of the degree of benefits and damages caused by the first as well as by the subsequent foreign loans. Those historians who maintain that foreign borrowing was to a certain degree beneficial to Greece argue that the loan of 1824 provided Greece with the impetus it needed to continue the war.[61] It was indeed a victory for it gave Greece some form of European recognition and reduced the country's feeling of isolation. A closer examination of the immediate and long term effects, both financial and political, will prove that there was only an illusion of benefit that the loan brought among some Greeks during the revolution.

The immediate consequences of the loan were that it intensified the tension among the existing factions who were eager to gain control of the

State Treasury.[62] The main division of factions as stated above was between the wealthy shipowners who allied themselves with the Phanariotes and the Kodja-Bashis of the mainland, and the chieftains, among whom Theodore Kolokotrones from the Morea was the most powerful. John Kolettes,[63] an Epirote doctor and Minister of War in the government, allied himself with the ruling elite of the Koundouriotes faction, and attempted to eliminate the Kolokotrones faction and take over Morea which the chieftains controlled. This was an effort to consolidate the Hydriot government's power in mainland Greece. During the early weeks of 1824 Kolettes employed troops from Northern Greece in order to fight Kolokotrones and secure hegemony for the provisional government.[64] When the news that a British loan was raised reached Greece, Kolettes was encouraged to wage a full scale war against the Moreates and Kolokotrones, one of the greatest Greek liberators.[65]

It is difficult, if not impossible, to estimate what portion of the first loan went for its intended purpose, namely, for military supplies and equipment designed to combat the Ottoman Turks. According to Professor Andreades, only a small portion served that purpose.[66] Negotiators, promoters and the Hydriot government absorbed the majority of the funds. The provisional government spent most of the loan money combating the political opposition in Morea. This was ironic since the Greeks contracted the loan in order to gain their independence from Turkey and not from each other. Apparently the Koundouriotes faction wanted to secure Greek independence under its own leaderhip only. One contemporary historian wrote concerning the uses and abuses of the first Greek loan:

The first sums[67] which arrived from England in 1824 were absorbed by arrears due on public and private debts. The payments made had no reference to the necessities of the public service, they were determined by the influence of individual members of the government. The greater part of the first loan was paid over to the shipowners and sailors of what was called the Greek fleet; the lion's share was appropriated to the Albanians[68] of Hydra and Spetzas.[69]

Considerable portions of the 1824 loan were absorbed by two civil wars (1823 to 1824) which were fought by the Koundouriotes faction against Kolokotrones and other Moreates chieftains who presented a political threat to the provisional government's hegemony in Greece.[70] The government used the loan to commission Roumeliotes and other northern Greek chieftains and captains and their men to eliminate the Peloponnesian political and military opposition.[71]

A recent study by Professor Anastasios Lignades entitled *The First Loan of Independence* has challenged the traditional historical views that the loan was abused by the Hellenic government. According to Lignades' research in 1824 the Greek naval force consisted of 90,100 boats. The government spent 170,000 pounds sterling annually to maintain these boats and an additional 31,875 pounds sterling for fifteen gun boats. The army's expenditure amounted to 2,444,000 grosia (100 grosia = 21.25 pounds sterling) for 51,000 men, and an additional 37,187 pounds sterling for 35,000 who served in 1824. The annual government expenditure in 1824 was 644,000 pounds sterling but the provisional government received from the first loan 298,726 pounds sterling. Lignades concludes, "where then is the waste of the first loan, when the sum received was less than the expenditure."[72] Certainly this is a convincing argument for who can deny the monumental expenses of the provisional government.

It would be a great omission, however, if the domestic loans, contributions from the philhellenes, income from rents of the National property, and confiscated Turkish wealth were not included in the 1824 public revenues.[73] In addition to the regular public revenues therefore, there was the loan of 1824 and also the above-mentioned funds. All of these resources for which no precise statistics exist were insufficient to cover the country's enormous expenditures. The issue before us, however, is not whether Greece suffered continuous deficits in the 1820s as a result of the War, but rather how the funds from the loan were allocated. The country's great deficit does not justify the abuses of the loan by the government. Money from the loan was mishandled and wasted by both the Greek army and the navy. In the army, personnel drew pay illegally and rations were drawn for troops who never served. Many *kapetanoi* (captains) sought the opportunity to become wealthy with the government loan. George Finlay wrote about one such individual who made fraudulent use of the government funds.

The English loans increased his (Makrys) treasures. . . . Yet
with all his wealth, he was in the habit of drawing pay and
rations for five hundred men, when he had only fifty under
his arms. [74]

Abuses also extended to the navy which was controlled by the wealthy
shipowners. The navy's vessels belonged to the Koundouriotes family and
the wealthy shipowning families of the islands of Hydra, Spetzas and
Psara. [75] The provisional government purchased a number of fireships
but they inflicted no loss on the Turkish fleet. [76]

Such abuses on all government levels cannot be ignored nor can it be
overlooked that the Koundouriotes faction used the loan to engage in civil
wars against the Moreates chieftains. The loan's most damaging effect,
however, did not stop with the fraudulent use of funds. Many Greeks
deceived themselves when they learned that the British offered financial
aid to a struggling nation. They regarded foreign financial aid as the
solution to their problem with Turkey and many abandoned their struggle. A contemporary historian wrote, "The streets for many months
were crowded with thousands of gallant young men in picturesque dresses
and richly ornamented arms, who ought to have been on the frontier
of Greece." [77] Such were the immediate negative results which the loan
of 1824 produced. In a later section the long term negative effects will
also be analyzed.

B.   The Loan of 1825

The Greek envoys in London, Louriotes and Orlandos, seized upon
the opportunity after their first success in 1824 to negotiate a second
loan. The British promoters and sponsors of the first Greek loan enthu-
siastically endorsed the proposal for a second loan. The reason for this
enthusiasm as one historian explained was due to the financiers' eagerness
"to secure commissions and quick profits and by manipulating the market
to keep at high levels the price of the standing bonds." [78] Indeed there
was no other motive behind the readiness of bankers and middlemen
to negotiate a loan other than profit. By early 1825 the London Greek
Committee faded away; it stopped its regular meetings and it did not
take an active role in Greek politics. [79] Philhellenism faded away in London but profiteering did not.

The reasons that the Greek delegates wished to negotiate another loan were twofold; first, to keep the Koundouriotes' government and the shipowners of the islands in power and second, to bind British financial interests to the Greek cause. On 1 February 1825, Louriotes wrote to L. Koundouriotes that the future of Greece depended upon the leaders of the islands of Hydra, Spetzas and Psaras.[80] It was clear from the delegation's dispatches to the provisional government that Louriotes' and Orlandos' primary concern was not the Turkish defeat but the achievement of this goal only with the Koundouriotes' family in power. The Hydriot government needed more money to continue bribing the Roumeliot captains and their forces whose only goal was to weaken and ultimately eliminate the Moreat political opposition.

Before they started loan negotiations, Louriotes and Orlandos advised Koundouriotes on 29 January 1825 to prepare a Hydriot ship with "wines from Samos and Santorine, olives, olive oil, raisins, lemons, etc. which would produce great results and would increase the pro-Greek fanaticism (in England)."[81] This sort of bribery was intended to create a favorable atmosphere among London financiers and politicians thus facilitating the Greek envoy's task. The Greek delegates did not stop with the "gifts," however, in their effort to gain favorable terms from London bankers. They attempted to create a competitive atmosphere among European banking houses so they went to Paris in search of a larger loan with better terms than they had secured in 1824. In France, the Paris Philhellenic Committee helped Orlandos and Louriotes to obtain an offer from a French bank for 10,000,000 francs at five percent interst, one percent sinking fund charge and fifty percent price of issue.[82] The British banking House of Ricardo Brothers offered Greece a loan of 2,000,000 pounds sterling at five percent interest one percent sinking fund and fifty-five and one half percent price of issue.[83] These terms were obviously more attractive to the Greek envoys and they accepted them.

On 7 February 1825, the Greek delegation signed the contract for the second loan in London. The price of issue was 1,100,000 pounds sterling, the maturing interest for the first two years at five percent amounted to 200,000 pounds sterling and the sinking fund charges at one percent totalled 20,000 pounds sterling for the same period. The promoters and negotiators received 68,800 pounds in commissions and the net sum available for the Hydriot government was 811,200 pounds sterling.[84] According to the contract the funds were remitted in twelve payments to Greece, not six as was the case for the first loan.[85] Once again Greece pledged the National property and its produce as a guarantee for the second time. As it will be shown in the next chapters, the Greek government paid dearly in the nineteenth century for pledging its entire National domains to British bondholders.

From the net amount of 811,200 pounds sterling the Greeks spent 392,000 for purchases of military supplies and equipment.[86] The Greek deputies in London ordered the purchase of eight frigates from the funds of the second loan.[87] Louriotes and Kondotavlos, a Chiote banker, ordered two of the eight frigates from the United States through the New York Philhellenic Committee.[88] According to the agreement between the Greeks and the American shipbuilders the cost of the frigates totalled 156,000 pounds sterling and the ships would be equiped with sixty-three cannons. The Americans, however, underestimated their cost and demanded an additional 50,000 pounds sterling to the agreed price. Otherwise they refused to deliver the order.[89] Finally, the Americans sent only one ship to Greece in November 1825, a few months later than they had promised[90] to deliver both vessels.

The London Greek Committee placed an order for six steamships on behalf of Greece in February 1825. The Committee placed 160,000 pounds sterling in Lord Cochrane's trust to carry out the burden of personally delivering the order to Greece.[91] Lord Cochrane was a philhellene but he chose to contribute to his own cause rather than the Greek so he pocketed 57,000 pounds sterling of the total sum placed in his trust.[92] Lord Cochrane agreed with the Greek Committee that the steamboats would be delivered to Greece by August 1825. One year after the agreed delivery date one steamship *Karteria* arrived in Greece to save the country from Ibrahim Pasha's Egyptian fleet.[93] The Greek deputies ordered the banking house of Ricardo not to issue any further sums to the contractors responsible for delivering the ships "and yet the sum of 123,000 pounds sterling had disappeared."[94] The Greeks therefore received two vessels of little value to their war effort, but paid dearly for both vessels.

From the 1,100,000 pounds sterling price of issue of the second loan the Greek government actually received 232,558 pounds sterling.[95] The rest went to profiteers. The London *Times* published an article on 28 November 1826, concerning the abuses of the first two Greek loans which accurately characterized and criticized the British plundering of the loan funds.

> . . .after the scandalous manner in which the Greeks have been plundered by a gang of humble knaves in this country, we do not know why that injured and unhappy people should not seek refuge in Royal protectors. May the money of which they have been robbed bring a curse upon those who possess it. May no Englishmen every repeat their names but with a shudder.[96]

These words are mild in comparison to the injury British profiteers caused to a nation struggling for its freedom. The best observation concerning the loans of insurgent Greece was made by Professor Andreades, who wrote extensively on the Greek foreign debt.

> Admittedly the history of the loans is one of the more painful in the pages of the Revolution. . .in spite of the scandals to which the loans gave birth, the financial problem (of Greece) was nevertheless successfully confronted; this was due to voluntary contributions. . . .He who wishes therefore to formulate a concise judgment concerning the finances of the Revolution, should admit that the Greek people on the one hand, readily in heavy sacrifice did its duty; the government however were more not in the height of their mission; as for the foreign capitalists, they either exploited us to a great extent or they helped us.[97]

This was indeed a just conclusion to draw concerning the Greek loans of 1824 and 1825, for it placed the responsibility for abuses on the Greek government as well as the British profiteers. As it will be seen in the third chapter the long-term effects of the first Greek loans had far more damaging consequences than those analyzed above.

C. *Foreign Borrowing During the Presidency*

In March 1827 the Greek National Assembly met to elect the first president of the Greek State, John Kapodistrias. Kapodistrias enjoyed an illustrious career in Russia in which he was foreign minister from 1815 to 1822.[98] When he arrived in Greece in January 1828 the country was in total chaos politically, economically and socially. As a result of the Greek-Turkish war the population declined from 875,150 in 1821 to 741,850 in 1828.[99] Besides the war against the Ottoman empire, the Greeks also suffered three civil wars, from November 1823 until August 1827[100] with intervals of peace. The country was socially, politically and economically disunited and only the common enemy, Turkey, kept the Greeks from weakening and disintegrating. The material resources of insurgent Greece were depleted by the long struggle and the people became increasinly more dependent upon foreign contributions. Finlay characterized the state of Greece as Kapodistrias found it in the following manner:

> During this period of destitution, which commenced towards the end of 1826 and continued until the harvest of 1828, the greater part of the Greeks who bore arms against the Turks were fed by Greek communities in Switzerland, France and Germany.[101]

Agriculture, business, commerce, industry and navigation which were the country's most important economic sectors were at a stage of stagnation and decay when Kapodistrias became president.[102] In 1820 the gross national product amounted to 100,000,000 gold drachmas and the public revenues were 30,000,000 drachmas; in 1828 the gross national product was reduced to 60,000,000 drachmas and the public revenues were 12,000,000 drachmas.[103] Kapodistrias was well aware of the nation's economic decadence and financial bankruptcy before he became president and he believed that the country's economic solution was agrarian reform. He wanted to break up the big landowning oligarchy in Greece and to distribute land to all those who wanted to farm.[104] Agrarian reforms, however, took time and the country needed immediate financial relief. The President realized this as he described the state of the Greek economy and finances below:

> The State has no finances. The mainland and Peloponnesus yield no revenue; and the revenues from the archipelago have

for the most part been exhausted . . . . The people are at their
last extremity; because the soldiers without fighting the Turks
are devouring their means of subsistence both for the present
and for the long future.[105]

The major economic setback as Kapodistrias realized was the non-utilization of the National property which could have yielded great wealth to the people and the government because of its vastness.

The total amount of arable land in Greece during the Presidency was 7,435,900 *stremata*; 5,800,000 *stremmata* were National Estates.[106] The total number of the Greek population during the same period was 741, 950.[107] Only eighty thousand to one hundred and fifty thousand owned land, out of an agricultural population which numbered half a million to six hundred thousand.[108] The vast majority of the Greeks were propertyless and no measures had been taken to solve this problem by the provisional government. The National Assembly of 1822 promised to grant one acre of land to every man who served in the military for each month of service. The National Assembly also passed legislation in April 1827, to reward plots of land to those who had served the country in the Revolutionary War.[109] No measures were actually taken, however, during the Revolution to adopt a course of massive land distributions for two reasons. First, the Greek governments, as much as they wished to be popular, realized that the National Estates could be used for contracting more foreign loans, and second, the National Lands and their produce were mortgaged to British bondholders for the first two loans, therefore they could not be alienated.

The immediate national interests required however that an efficient utilization method should have been found for the National property whose total value in 1830 amounted to 502,400,400 gold drachmas,[110] a substantial amount which could have solved some economic and financial difficulties for Greece. P. N. Lidorikes, the minister of finance during the Presidency, reported to Kapodistrias that the mainland did not yield any revenues to the Public Treasury and that except for an insignificant amount collected from the islands, the government had expenses only and no revenue.[111] The table on the following page provides a clear indication of the Greek economic decline during the Revolution from the three main sectors which yielded receipts to the Public Treasury.

Year	Peloponnesus	Sterea	Islands[112]
1825	3,903,470 gr.	645,110 gr.	1,040,930 gr.
1826	274,727 gr.	397,700 gr.	978,055 gr.
1827	847 gr.	16,025 gr.	769,108 gr.

Kapodistrias inherited an empty treasury, a large expenditure, and an even larger foreign debt. Before he took power he realized that in order to immediately stimulate the decadent Greek economy, to organize and stabilize the government he needed to resort to foreign loans.

In his attempt to raise European loans, Kapodistrias encountered a number of problems. France and Great Britain distrusted him because of his former ties with the Russian government.[113] After the Duke of Wellington replaced George Canning, the Foreign Office suspected that Kapodistrias "was a tool of Russian diplomacy."[114] Even though this was not true, it was true that the Greek President symphized with the Russians and they in return supported him.[115] Besides these obstacles which alienated the President from the Western European nations and limited his opportunities of securing a loan from them, there was another problem. The wasteful spending of the first two loans, and the Greek government's default on the interest payments to the bondholders created an unfavorable atmosphere in Western Europe for Kapodistrias or any Greek statesmen to raise another foreign loan.

In spite of the overwhelming odds against him the President went to London and Paris in search of financial support. He was unable, however, to impress either the French or the British to provide any financial assistance for Greece.[116] Kapodistrias asked for 2,000,000 pounds sterling guaranteed loan from the three Powers and early in 1828, Russia offered to guarantee a third share of the proposed amount[117] but the two Western Powers declined to secure the remaining. Kapodistrias did not remain inactive awaiting for the Powers to reconsider his proposal. He established a Greek National Bank in which 525,000 francs were deposited.[118] Many American and European philhellenic societies also contributed a sizeable sum of 2,513,000 francs to Greece in 1827. Furthermore the President appealed to Tsar Nicholas I for financial aid and Russia which was more than anxious to gain political influence in Greece contributed 3,500,000 rubles to the Greek Public Treasury from 1828 to 1830. Nicholas I also supplied Greece with guns and ammunition and persuaded the French government to contribute 6,000,000 francs to the desperate nation.[119] Great Britain also gave 500,000 francs in 1831 after Kapodistrias' assassination.[120]

The President never achieved his goal of raising 60,000,000 francs, but he was able to stimulate some economic growth with the foreign aid which he secured during his presidency. Public revenue was raised from 785,980 grosia in 1827 to 4,655,956 in the second six month period of the 1828 fiscal year. From February 1828 to April 1829 the revenues reached 8,530,000 and the following fiscal year they were up to 12,387,000.[121] Inspite of the enormous financial improvements during the presidency Greece suffered repeated deficits. "In 1828 revenue covered just over 30 percent of expenditure; in 1829 just over 40 percent; in 1830 almost 50 percent and in 1831 over 55 percent."[122] The insoluble financial difficulties of Greece according to Professor Andreades could have been resolved by foreign loans.[123] This indeed would have been a temporary solution but with drastic long-term political and financial effects in Greece. The expansion of the Greek foreign debt gave cause to the Great Powers to interfere in the domestic affairs of Greece after the guaranteed loan of 1832 was contracted. Furthermore, more foreign loans would have given cause to the Greeks to abandon their own efforts to resolve the economic and financial problems facing them.

Kapodistrias, like the provisional government before him, did not succeed in regenerating the Greek economy and making proper use of the National Estates and this was the reason for the country's continued financial and economic weaknesses. The National Bank which the President set up did not remain a stable financial institution in Greece because the deposited funds were nothing more than "a forced loan" which the government extorted from the people.[124] It cannot seriously be argued therefore that Kapodistrias had honest intentions about long-term economic developments since he did not implement any measures toward that goal. The President's government did very little to encourage trade, commerce and industry which would have contributed considerably to the national wealth.[125]

In the agricultural sector Kapodistrias tried to introduce various methods of improvement to increase production, but he failed.[126] He established institutes of agriculture in a nation which had no schools of any sort and illiteracy among the agrarian population was extremely high. He distributed some land to the very poor,[127] but he did not take effective measures to deal with the problem of the propertyless agrarian population. The result of his failure to distribute land to the people was widespread brigandage.[128] Thousands of Greeks who fought the Turks during the Revolution found themselves without any possessions or skills to utilize and once there was peace in Greece these men turned to the life of looting, kidnapping and killing for survival. The Kapodistrian government never gave them an alternative to the only life-style they knew.

The provisional governments of Greece as well as Kapodistrias' did very little to relieve the people's economic misery. The Hellenic governments from 1821 to 1831 plunged the country into debts and contributed to its political divisions. It is true that there was little any government could have accomplished under the revolutionary conditions which confronted Greece during the 1820s. It is also true, however, that these governments were more concerned with retaining power than they were with resolving the country's economic and financial difficulties.

CHAPTER II

THE GUARANTEED LOAN AND THE GREAT POWERS

A.   The Guaranteed Loan of 1832

On 6 July 1827, France, Russia and Great Britain signed a treaty in London to end hostilities between Greece and the Ottoman empire.[1] This treaty was the first major step by the Great Powers to recognize Greece as an independent state. During the Kapodistrias presidency the Powers were in search of an European prince who was willing to become the first Greek monarch. In 1830 their search ended when they agreed to select Prince of Saxe-Coburg Leopold.[2] The Powers informed Leopold that he was their choice to become the first king of Greece. Before he formally accepted the candidacy for the throne Prince Leopold placed a number of demands before the Powers for which he required their fulfillment as a precondition to his acceptance of the Greek Crown.

Most of Leopold's demands were financial but he also made territorial demands which the Ottoman empire would have been forced by the Powers to concede. The Prince knew that the future kingdom of Greece which the Powers asked him to rule needed Europe's guaranteed financial support until its economy developed sufficiently to yield the necessary revenues for the government. Great Britain did not intend to give any financial aid to Leopold nor was she willing to guarantee a loan to Greece.[3] On 10 February 1830, the Duke of Wellington informed Prince Leopold that the Great Powers would not yield to his financial demands. The British Prime Minister wrote to Leopold:

I must beg your Grace will be in your Answer to this point (concerning financial aid) very explicit as I understand that the Provisional government has, until now, only existed by Foreign subsidies which I am told are from hence to cease.[4]

Prince Leopold had influential friends in the British parliament who trusted him and wished to see that his financial requests from the Powers were met. Furthermore, the Foreign Office feared French and Russian political influence in Greece and in view of British diplomatic isolation Wellington retracted his original position.[5]

On 20 February 1830, the three European Powers signed a protocol by which they agreed to guarantee a loan for Greece. According to the protocol the Greek government would raise the loan for the purpose of maintaining a military force essential to the sovereign's safety and to the country's tranquility.[6] Three days after the Powers signed the agreement for the guaranteed loan, Leopold accepted the offer to become the first Greek monarch. On 10 March 1830, the Prince asked that the amount for the guaranteed loan should be 60,000,000 francs.[7] Lord Aberdeen, Wellington's foreign secretary, thought that 60,000,000 francs was too large a price for the Powers to pay and recommended that Great Britain wanted to guarantee separately from the other Powers 500,000 pounds sterling, or 12,500,000 francs.[8] According to Aberdeen the British loan should "be advanced in seven yearly instalments, leaving the other Powers separately to guarantee their respective quotas."[9] Leopold was totally dissatisfied with the Aberdeen proposal and he threatened to withdraw his candidacy if his terms were not met.[10] Confronted with that threat the Foreign Office fully consented to Leopold's financial requests.
fronted with that threat the Foreign Office fully consented to Leopold's financial requests.

The Prince felt the weight of his bargaining position and requested that the instalments on the loan should not be granted by fixed periods as the Powers wanted, but according to the Greek government's financial needs.[11] Furthermore, Leopold asked that the Powers should force the Ottoman Empire to make certain territorial concessions to Greece.[12] The Powers wanted to negotiate the terms of the loan with the Prince but they refused to carve up any Turkish territories to satisfy Greece and its future sovereign.[13] On 21 May 1830, Leopold resigned his sovereignty and the Powers once again were in search of a candidate for the Greek throne.

The next candidate for the Greek throne was Prince Frederic Otho of Bavaria, second son of King Ludwig.[14] Otho was only seventeen years of age when the Powers selected him in May 1832 so his father, Ludwig, acted as his son's representative in negotiations with the Powers. Ludwig asked the Powers to guarantee Greece a loan of 60,000,000 francs, but unlike Leopold, the Bavarian king did not demand any territorial concessions from the Ottoman empire.[15] Russia, France and England agreed to guarantee the 60,000,000 francs loan to Greece and on 7 May 1832, a treaty was signed between the Great Powers and Bavaria thereby establishing the kingdom of Greece.[16]

Article XII of the Treaty dealt with the loan of 60,000,000 francs and specified the reciprocal financial obligations between the Greek kingdom and the Powers. The first two clauses of Article XII stated that the Powers guaranteed a loan of 60,000,000 francs to Greece which would be raised in three instalments at 20,000,000 francs each. The third and fourth clauses stated that the first instalment would be raised immediately and the remaining instalments would be raised according to the kingdom's necessities after agreement between the Powers and the Greek monarch.[17] The fifth and sixth clauses were the most important ones because the Powers used them as the legal foundation to intervene into Greek internal affairs and exercise financial influence which at certain times amounted to financial control. The paragraphs stated:

(5) In the event of the second and third instalments of the above mentioned loan being raised in consequence of such an agreement, the three Courts shall each become responsible for the payment of one-third of the annual amount of the interest and sinking fund of these two instalments, as well as of the first.

(6) The Sovereign of Greece and the Greek State shall be bound to appropriate to the payment of the interest and sinking fund of such instalment of the Loan as may have been raised under the guarantee of the three Courts, the first revenues of the State, in such manner that the actual receipts of the Greek Treasury shall be devoted *first of all,* to the payment of the said interest and sinking fund, and shall not be employed for any other purpose, until those payments on account of the instalments of the loan raised under the guarantee of the three Courts, shall have been completely secured for the current year. The diplomatic representatives of the Three Courts in Greece shall be specially

charged to watch over the fulfillment of the last-mentioned stipulation.[18]

The sixth clause of Article XII laid the foundations for European financial control in Greece. There was nothing in the Treaty which suggested what action the Powers would take in the event Greece failed to discharge her financial obligations toward them. The Treaty did enable the Powers, however, to take any course of action which they all agreed upon in case the protectorate failed to respond to the Treaty's terms.

A. M. Andreades and J. Levandes who have studied the Greek foreign debt of the nineteenth century ascertain that the Powers never took steps to control Greek finances even though Article XII gave them that power.[19] This is true to a certain degree only. The Great Powers never took total financial control in Greece but they did exercise a certain degree of control during King Otho's reign as will be shown in the next chapters.

The new Greek sovereign's representatives insisted that the Powers should submit the entire sum of the loan at once and not just a third of it as stiplulated by the Treaty. The Powers refused to grant Otho this concession and the fourth clause of Article XII remained unaltered.[20] On 1 May 1833, Greece contracted the guaranteed loan with the banking house of the Rothschild Brothers in Paris. The price of issue was ninety-four percent, at five percent interest annually and one percent sinking fund charge.[21] The 60,000,000 francs or 64,000,000 drachmas was reduced considerably after commissions, fees and interest charges were paid. From May 1833 to 31 December 1843, interest and sinking fund charges consumed 33,000,000 drachmas from the loan. From the remaining 24,000,000 drachmas Greece compensated the Ottoman empire 12,531,000 drachmas for territorial concessions which the Turks rewarded to Greece. The table on the following page specifies how the series A and B—two-thirds of the loan—were allocated.

As the table indicates, only a small part of the first two instalments from the loan remained for the Public Treasury. Prince Otho and his Bavarian entourage were responsible for some serious abuses of the loan funds. The Powers, however, also contributed to misappropriation of loan funds. They forced the country to compensate the Ottoman empire for Attica, Euboia and Fthiotida, all of which were territories which the Greeks liberated.

Table of A and B Series of the Guaranteed Loan[22]

Profit of the issued loan to the House
    of Rothschild . . . . .4,945,761.60 drachmas
Interest for 1833-35. . . . . .7,600,000.00 drachmas
The President's debt to Eynard . . . . 276,771.00 drachmas
Debts of the three Powers. . . . . .1,962,407.24 drachmas
Compensation to Turkey for the granting of Attica,
    Euboia and part of Fthiotida . . . . 12,531,238.40 drachmas
Travelling expenses to members of the Bavarian
    Regency . . . . 422,207.20 drachmas
Travelling expenses to Bavarian administrative
    personnel. . . . . 163,545.20 drachmas
Wages to members of Regency . . . . .1,409,000.00 drachmas
Moving expenses for Otho's escorted military 1,656,703.28 drachmas
Recruiting and moving expenses for the Bavarian
    Volunteer Corps . . . . .3,330,171.00 drachmas
Purchase of military supplies . . . . 910,607.00 drachmas
Royal nomismatopoisis. . . . . 459,728.52 drachmas
TOTAL. . . . . .35,668,141.35 drachmas
Subtracted from the Principal of A and B
    series. . . . . 44,670,000.00 drachmas
Remainder for the domestic
    service to Greece . . . . .9,001,858.65 drachmas

The armed Bavarian Voluntary Corps of 3,500 men[23] cost the Greek government a total of 5,897,481 drachmas. This expense was absolutely unnecessary because Greece had a most capable military force of its own. When Otho arrived at Nauplion, the old capital of Greece before Athens, the majority of the nine thousand men who served in the military during the Kapodistrian presidency were dismissed. These highly trained and low-paid men were replaced by highly-paid Bavarian soldiers who did not have military expertise in Greece. The men who fought to liberate their nation were forced out of their own military and were expected to pay taxes in order to sustain a foreign military force. The consequences of the military displacement of Greeks with Bavarians were disastrous.

Many displaced soldiers and officers turned to brigandage because they had no possessions or alternative occupations.[24] Brigandage remained a major force in Greece throughout Otho's thirty-year reign.[25]

The second loan abuse cost Greece 12,531,000 drachmas. The Powers and the Sublime Porte agreed that this sum should be rewarded to the latter as compensation for certain Turkish occupied territories of Southeastern Greece. The Greeks felt that they had compensated the Sublime Porte with their blood and had rightfully won those territories.[26]

The remaining sum of the A and B series was insubstantial to sustain the large bureaucracy which the Bavarians created in Greece. In February 1835 the British representative at Athens, E.J. Dawkins, informed the Foreign Office that the funds from the first two loan instalments were completely exhausted.[27] In June 1835, Spyridon Trikoupis, the Greek ambassador to London, informed the Power's Plenipotentiaries that Greece urgently needed an advance of 3,000,000 francs on the third instalment.[28] Viscount Palmerston,[28 a] Lord Grey's foreign secretary, raised immediate objections to Trikoupis' request. He refused to consider submitting the entire third instalment or even an advance on it as Greece requested. The other two guaranteeing governments agreed with the Foreign Office.

The Powers decided that:

> ... before they could consent that their respective Courts should guarantee the third instalment, it would be necessary that the Greek government should show what steps it has taken to appropriate, as required by the Treaty, the first produce of the Revenues of the Greek State to the payment of the interest of the loan.[29]

The Greek Minister of Finance, H.G. Theocharis, provided the Powers upon their request with a complete exposé of the Greek revenues and expenditures for the years 1833 and 1834. He also presented the budgets of 1835 and 1836.

Year	Revenues	Expenditures	Defecit[30]
1833	7,042,653.30	13,630,467.42	6,587,814.12
1834	9,455,410.07	20,150,657.33	10,695,247.26
1835	10,737,011.36	16,851,070.04	6,114,058.68
1836	11,312,445.00	15,333,955.00	4,021,510.00

The Bavarian Court's inability to reduce the Treasury's defecits did not only sink the country deeper into debt but also resulted in the government's incapability to solve the growing social disorders.

In the winter of 1834 and spring of 1835 social disorders escalated to such an alarming number that the threat of revolution was real. Greek rebels killed several Bavarians, looted stores and took money from the government sources.[31] The revolts directly threatened the Bavarian Court in Athens and the Regent, Count Armansperg, a despotic ruler whom the Greeks hated. The Count and many others in the government were greatly alarmed by the social disturbances. The British Legation at Athens was also alarmed by the rising brigandage and wished to protect Count Armansperg who favored British diplomacy in Greece. Sir Edmund Lyons, the British minister in Greece who replaced Dawkins, wrote to Lord Palmerston in the spring of 1836 that the government in Athens desperately needed the third instalment if it was expected to survive and supress brigandage. Lyons assessed the Greek revolts for the Foreign Office as follows:

> . . . the leaders of the insurgents have undoubtedly money at their command, whilst the measures of government are cramped for want of it; immediate relief must be granted. The rebels say "the government has no money and can only obtain it by imposing taxes on the Mereots, which will make them discontented and disposed to join us.[32]

Palmerston had a political ally in the Greek Court, Armansperg, and as long as the Regent was in power England could exert maximum influence in Greece.[33]

The Russian and the French governments knew of course about England's political influence in the Greek Court and resented it.[34] They hoped to diminish British influence in Greece by patronizing the Greek political parties named after the three Powers. The parties represented the political ideology of the Protecting Powers and each party believed that Greece's best interests would be served by their patron Power. The French government supported the "French" faction with John Kolettes as its leader, the Russian government supported the "Russian" faction with Theodore Kolokotrones and Andrew Metaxas as its most nominent leaders.[35] Since Greece was rule by a Regent despotically, the three political parties did not have much influence in the government.[36] Palmerston had a distinct advantage over the other two Powers since Amansperg was pro-British. Great Britain therefore had an interest to grant the third instalment of the loan whereas the other two guaranteeing governments did not.

In November 1835, the Greek Public Treasury had 70,842 drachmas remaining from the A and B series of the loan.[37] In April 1836 Palmerston urged the Russians and the French to cooperate with his government in submitting the third instalment to Greece. He met in a conference with H. Sebastiani, the French representative in London, and Pozo di Borgo, Russian ambassador in England, to review the Greek state of affairs and to consider the possibility of granting the third instalment to the protectorate. Both the French and the Russian representatives opposed Palmerston's recommendation to submit the entire third instalment to Greece. Count di Borgo maintained that his government authorized him to grant an advance of 1,212,000 francs from the third instalment. This sum was sufficient to pay "Mssrs. Rothchild the amount issued by them in March last (1836) for the divedents and sinking fund of the first two instalments."[38] France was much more generous than Russia. Adolphe Thiers, instructed Sebastiani in London to guarantee Greece an advance of 5,000,000 francs on the remainder of the third instalment.[39] Palmerston attempted to persuade Thiers of the urgent Greek financial needs and suggested to the French statesman that the Powers should advance 10,000,000 francs. Thiers, however, did not comply. In June Palmerston once again tried to convince Count di Borgo of the Powers' obligation to provide the third instalment for their protectorate based on its needs.[40] The Russian Ambassador remained unyielding to British pleas and criticized the Greek government for its failure to fulfill its financial obligations towards the Rothchild Bank.[41]

Palmerston decided to act without French and Russian cooperation. In July he appeared before the House of Commons and persuaded the British representative to guarantee Greece Britain's one-third of the third instalment without the other two Powers' cooperation on this matter.[42] On 19 August 1836, the Parliament passed a bill which gave Palmerston the authority to remit Britain's share of the third instalment without conferring with Russia or France.[43]

The Bavarian Court in Greece knew that while England wished to remit the third instalment the French and the Russian governments refused to cooperate with Palmerston. A year before the British Parliament passed a bill which authorized Palmerston to grant Great Britain's share of the instalment, the Regency at Athens authorized the ango-phile Alexander Mavrokordatos to negotiate a loan from Bavaria.[44] Mavrokordatos and King Ludwig's government worked out a loan contract in June 1835 and the agreement was signed by Otho in September.[45] According to the Articles of agreement the Bavarian kingdom issued a loan to Greece because of the financial and social crisis which confronted the Greek Court. The guarantee for the Bavarian loan was the third instalment of the guaranteed loan of 1832 which was at the time still in the hands of the Rothchild Bank. The Bavarian loan was 496,665 gold fiorins or 1,000,000 francs, at four percent annual interest rate, and it was contracted by the Banking House of Baron Eichthal.[46] King Ludwig's government agreed to remit the sum of the loan on 10 October 1835, and after the Powers had granted the third instalment to Greece, the Regency at Athens would use the necessary funds to repay the Bavarian loan by October 1836. On 10, 23 March 1936, Bavaria further agreed to lend an additional 496,665 fiorins to the Greek monarch[47] under the same terms of the first loan.

The Bavarian loan was designed to bail out the king in time of crisis. Ludwig wanted to see an end to brigandage which presented a threat to his son's throne. The 1835 and 1836 loans, like the first two loans and the loan of 1832, had negative effects on Greece during Otho's reign. The Hellenic government increased its debt since Otho's reign enormously and it defaulted its payments on all foreign loans.

B.   *Palmerston and the Greek Foreign Debt, 1837-1850*

During the years of the Armansperg regime, July 1934 to February 1837, the Foreign Office enjoyed great influence in Greek politics.[48] This was the only reason that Palmerston granted Greece financial aid while Russia and France opposed such course of action. British influence in Athens came to an abrupt end, however, on 2 February 1837 when Otho returned to Greece with his bride Amalia.[49] The King returned to his Court with renewed confidence about his position in the realm and in an effort to consolidate power into his own hands he dismissed Count Armansperg.[50] Otho appointed, for a brief period of ten months Ignaz von Rudhart as Prime Minister and thereafter took power into his own hands and ruled Greece as an absolute monarch until the September Revolution of 1843.[51]

Armansperg's fall from power and Otho's opposition to Alexander Mavrokordatos, an anglo-phile, as well as all pro-British elements from government, changed British foreign policy in Greece.[52] Palmerston and Lyons altered their favorable attitude toward Greece and started to publicly criticize King Otho as a despotic ruler.[53] British foreign policy in Athens remained hostile until Otho's exile in 1862. On the other hand, Otho's anti-British policy never changed during his reign. In order to minimize British antagonism in Athens, the Greek monarch turned to his father, Ludwig, and asked him to use his offices in European courts so that the Greek state could be free from foreign interference.[54] Otho used his father's offices throughout his reign to prevent the Powers from interfering in Greek domestic affairs.

Anglo-Greek relations rapidly deteriorated when Otho dismissed Rudhart and reserved the office of the Prime Minister for himself.[55] The decline of British influence in Athens cleared the way for the Russians and the French, who were discontent ever since 1833 with the Greek Court, to patronize Court and government. The following exerpt from a Foreign Office memorandum reveals the British position concerning French influence in Greek politics after the Rudhart dismissal.

> In March 1838 France adopted a new course, for she was anxious to obtain a political influence in Greece, and she thought that that could be effected by paying the interest due as her portion in money, and retaining the bonds of the third series still in her possession, since she would thus be a direct creditor upon Greece for the sum issued in the first instance, and would possess a large sum in hand in the shape of the bonds in question (to advance or not, at any time, according to the conduct which the Greek government might pursue towards that of this country) in the second.[56]

The exerpt above clearly shows that financial relations between Greece and the Powers were determined on the basis of diplomatic considerations. Idologically Otho leaned more towards autocratic Russia than liberal France and England so after 1838 he adopted a Russophile policy.[57] In view of the Greek Court's change in policy, Palmerston and Louis-Philippe demanded that Greece met her financial obligations toward the guaranteeing governments. Both France and England had serious doubts about the Greek government's ability to liquidate her foreign debt, and they feared that they would be ultimately forced by the Treaty of 1832 to discharge their Protectorate's financial obligations.[58]

The Powers' apprehensions concerning Greece's inability to pay her foreign debt were not unfounded. From 1833 to 1843 Greece suffered a deficit of 20,690,775 drachmas. The public revenues for the first ten years of Othonian rule were 138,412,648.94 drachmas while the expenditure for the same period was 159,103,424.23 drachmas.[59] As a result of such an enormous deficit the Greek government did not pay the interest and sinking fund during the decade of the 1830s to the Powers, nor did she pay any interest to Bavaria or to the British bondholders. Payments to the Powers were due twice a year on 1 March and 1 September. In February 1841 Greece informed the guaranteeing governments that it would begin payments on the interest in March of that year. For the first time the Greek government kept its word and discharged its financial obligations to the Powers from 1841 until 1843.[60] Up to March 1842 Greece had paid in interest and sinking fund charges to the Rothchild Bank 600,000 francs out of a total 1,665,306 francs which she owed in arrears. The Powers, however, had not paid Greece the entire third instalment of the loan so the Hellenic government could always rely on it to repay part of its foreign debt.[61]

In 1843 Greece suspended payments to the Powers because a revolution interrupted the government's normal financial affairs. The Revolution was carried out by military officers and politicians who wanted an end to Othonian absolutism and Bavarian domination of the Greek government. It was a bloodless affair which took place in Athens and it was resolved peacefully ending a decade of despotic rule.[62] The king had little choice but to accept the Constitution imposed upon him by the rebels since he had few supporters in Greece and even fewer in Europe.[63]

On 18 March 1844 Greece officially became a Constitutional Monarchy with an appointed Senate and an elected Parliament (*Boule*).[64]

In May 1843 Sir Robert Peel, the British Prime Minister, and Lord Palmerston complained before the House of Commons that the Greek government had failed to keep up with its payments on the interest of the guaranteed loan.[65] The Russian government was equally dissappointed with the Greeks for their neglect to dissolve their foreign debt. Count Nesselrode, Russian foreign minister, instructed the Russian representative in Athens, to remind the Greek government of its financial obligations to the Powers.[66] France, Russia and Great Britain met in a joint session in August 1843 to discuss the course of action which they should adopt to deal with Greece in regards to the loan. They concluded that the Hellenic government should be required "to make provision for the future payment of the loan out of its own resources and to indemnify this country (England) and the other Powers for the temporary advance they had made under the Treaty."[67] The Powers recommended that the expenditure on the Greek military should be decreased, that the National Estates be made productive to yield revenue for the government, and that a council should be established to review the annual budget and to remedy existing financial weaknesses in the country.[68]

The Greek government responded to the Powers that it was unable to pay the interest due on the loan but it proposed to raise another guaranteed loan to pay the arrears on that of 1832.[69] The three guaranteeing governments recommended that the solution to the Protectorate's financial situation was the application of administrative reforms.[70] The concerted financial pressures by the Powers which took place before the September 1843 Revolution and the domestic discontent with the monarchy were responsible for the success of the Constitutional Revolution.

The success of the Revolution quickly came to an end, however, in August 1844 when Otho disregarded the Constitution and selected John Kolettes to be his Prine Minister.[71] Kolettes, the leader of the "French" party, was distined to become the first dictator of the Greek kingdom. He was a loyal supporter of the Bavarian Court in Athens and he despised the British, sufficient qualifications from Otho's point of view to make him Prime Minister.[72] Kolettes shared the King's mistrust and hatred for Lyons and Palmerston and he entertained an expansionist foreign policy which appealed to the Greek King and Queen.[73]

The Foreign Office wanted a pro-British Cabinet in Athens but Otho disappointed them by appointing Kolettes who was pro-French. As a result of this factor Palmerston waged a diplomatic war on Greece from 1844 until 1850 when he ordered a naval blockade of Greece. France, however, enjoyed cordial relations with Greece and protected the Kolettes regime from Palmerston's antagonism.[74] Before Kolettes took power Great Britain and France, whose Near Eastern policy was in agreement after the second Mohamed Ali crisis of 1840,[75] acted jointly to force the Greek government to liquidate its foreign debt. In February 1844 Lord Aberdeen expressed his concern about the Greek foreign debt and the Protectorate's arrears due to the Powers which amounted to 700,000 drachmas.[76] Lyons was instructed by the Foreign Office to remind Greece before March 1844 not to neglect the instalment payment on the interest and the sinking fund.[77] Theobald Piscatory, the French minister at Athens, also reminded the Greek Foreign Ministry of her financial obligations to the Powers, and demanded satisfaction.[78]

The Franco-phile government in Athens, however, was responsible for the change in financial relations between Greece and France. After Kolettes took power in August the French Legation at Athens did not only stop to demand payment for the charges on the loan but defended the Cabinet against British hostilities. Piscatory, authorized by François Guizot who was a personal friend of Kolettes, patronized the "French" party in Greece and openly engaged in confrontations with the British Legation.[79] To counter the French offensive in Greece the Foreign Office used financial pressure tactics against the Hellenic government. On 31 July 1845, Lord Aberdeen appeared before the House of Commons to express his bitterness against the Greek government. He told the Parliament that:

> We have also guaranteed the payment of the interest of a loan contracted by the Greek State which we have been called upon to discharge ourselves for the last two or three years. This therefore, gives us undoubtedly a right to *interfere so far in the internal affairs of this State* as to see that we should be released from these obligations as rapidly as possible.[80]

This was a blunt public statement by a British official who declared for the first time since Greek independence that a European Power had the right to violate the sovereignty of the Greek State.

Two months after Aberdeen's public speech on Greek affairs, the British Foreign Secretary instructed Lyons to formally protest against the Kolettes administration's failure to pay the installment charges on the interest and sinking fund due to the Powers on 1 September 1845. Aberdeen advised Lyons that Greece violated the Treaty of 1832 but Britain wished to be moderate toward the Protectorate kingdom and allow it at least to use the surplus revenues for the loan's repayment.[81] As British pressure mounted, Kolettes announced in December 1845 that his administration would take decisive steps "to enforce a severe economy and by creating new resources, to seek the means of discharging their obligations."[82] Kolettes' promises never materialized and Greece continued to default during his stay in office. To make matters worse for Greece, Otho antagonized the British Legation at Athens[83] and as a result of this factor Lyon's reports to the Foreign Office concerning Greek affairs were partially prejudiced by his relations with the king. The House of Commons therefore pressured Greece to settle her foreign debt with the Powers.[84]

In the beginning of 1846 Anglo-Greek financial as well as foreign relations deteriorated considerably. One reason for this deterioration between the two countries relations was due to a much publicized financial report presented by the Greek Minister of Finance, M. Poniropoulos, to the Chamber of Deputies. Poniropoulos tactlessly announced to the Greek Parliament that:

> . . . the finances were entirely paralyzed and were plundered by
> everyone; that he (Poniropoulos) received no reports relative
> to the revenue; that he did not know the results of any financial
> operation; that he was therefore unable to draw up any draft of
> a budget.[85]

This report was published in the Greek newspapers and it obviously contradicted Kolettes' statement of December 1845 concerning Greek finances.

The Prime Minister was eager to defend himself and denounce Poniropoulos' account on the state of finances. Kolettes composed a lengthy report addressed to the Powers in which he explained the reasons for the administration's inability to meet its instalment payments. He wrote that it was his understanding that according to the Treaty of 1832 the guaranteed loan was intended to aid the Greek population, by improving its industry, commerce, agriculture and public services. The State's expenses, however, were so great, Kolettes continued, that during the first years of Otho's regency the Treasury suffered consecutive deficits.[86]

To a certain degree Kolettes was right about the enormous State expenditure. He did not explain, however, how the State Revenues were alocated. He clearly implied in his report that the reason Greece was unable to pay the interest, was due to the country's expenditure on public services, development of agriculture, commerce, industry and navigation. This was not the case at all. Kolettes who had dreams of expanding Greece territorially at Turkey's expense used most of the public revenues to build up the country's military. The budget of 1846 below clearly shows how the state funds were alocated.

1846 Budget-Expenditure[87]

Ministry of Foreign Affairs	498,731 drachmas
Ministry of Justice	875,431 drachmas
Ministry of the Interior	1,790,935 drachmas
Ministry of Public Instruction and Worship	873,026 drachmas
Ministry of Finance	439,480 drachmas
Ministry of the Navy	1,134,725 drachmas
Ministry of War	4,429,952 drachmas
Total	10,042,280 drachmas

The above table does not reflect the total budget of 1846 but it shows that the Kolettes administration used 5,564,677 drachmas for military build up and only 4,477,603 for the other five ministries.

The British Minister at Athens had no reason to believe Kolettes' justifications for the poor state of Greek finances. He informed the Greek Foreign Minister in March that Great Britain expected the Kolettes administration to meet the March and September payments due on the interest and sinking fund.[88] Greece did not make any payments to the Powers in 1846 but the Chamber of Deputies met on 6 October 1846 and proposed to use the surplus revenues of 1845, estimated at a minimum of 700,000 drachmas, to pay the interest and sinking fund to Russia and Great Britain.[89] Even if Greece submitted the 700,000 drachmas to the Powers for the debt it was an insignificant sum. In December 1846 the Government owed 79,905,114.33 drachmas on her foreign debt and 5,841,526.35 drachmas for interest on the auxiliary debt.[90]

During Kolettes' two years in office, Greece had not made any payments to the Powers. France did not complain but the other two Powers did and Kolettes wanted to convince them that the Greek economy was in a poor state. He designed a twenty-seven page report which he addressed to Persiany, the Russian minister at Athens, and Lyons with the intent to familiarize the two representatives with the true state of the Greek finances. In the laborious report the Prime Minister explained that Greece had limited economic resources and a great deal of expenses since it was a newly organized State. He defended the nation's military expenditure against British charges that Greece spent too much on military build up. Kolettes ascertained that a strong military force was vital to the nation's needs for keeping order against the threat of the ever growing brigandage which spread throughout Greece. He also defended the expenditure of the vast bureaucracy which was responsible for absorbing a good deal of the revenue. Finally, he presented his views on the undeveloped National Lands which were in his opinion a potential source of revenue and assured Lyons and Persiany that his Cabinet had honest intentions concerning the liquidation of the Greek foreign debt.[91]

A few days after Kolettes sent the above report to the Russian and British Legations at Athens, the Greek Minister of Finance, Poniropoulos, who embarrassed Kolettes in February 1846 by his public report on Greek finances, succeeded once again in February 1847 in accomplishing the same goal. On 3 February Poniropoulos delivered a public speech concerning the deplorable state of Greek finances. He explained the chaotic situation of the Greek financial administration as follows:

> I cannot gentlemen, conceal from you any longer the truth, the robbery of the public revenues has surpassed all measures, and is carried on with an insane prudence. But is this not the fault of the Minister? I hardly know fifty employees out of the thousands who belong to my department; if each steals a small portion of the revenue, the dimunition must naturally become

considerable. Things have arrived at such a pitch that it is impossible for the Minister of Finance to put a check to the abuses.[92]

Kolettes labored intensely to convince the Powers that the causes for Greek financial difficulties were not due to the government's corruption and maladministration but to the economic weaknesses and needs of the country. His own Minister of Finance, however, continued to contradict him.

The contradictory reports concerning Greek finances within the Kolettes administration gave Palmerston cause to increase British diplomatic pressure in Athens. Kolettes was fortunate, however, to have the French support which countered British policy in Greece. Guizot and the French Legation at Athens disregarded embezelments by Greek officials which according to Poniropoulos were the reason for budget deficits. Palmerston, however, insisted that such widespread government corruption was the cause behind the Greek government's default.[93] The British officials believed that the Franco-phile Cabinet at Athens made secret payments to France for the charges on the loan and this was the reason that France did not complain about Greek defaults as did Russia and Great Britain.[94] There is no evidence to support British suspicions that Greek secret payments to France ever took place. It was unlikely that the Kolettes administration which suffered consecutive budget deficits made payments to France. The British knew this but they wanted to made a political issue out of it exposing French interference in Greek affairs.

On 1 March 1847, Greece defaulted her payments again and Palmerston was enraged with Kolettes for his conduct toward the Powers. He wrote to Lyons that Greek finances under the Kolettes regime continued to deteriorate, that financial abuses escalated and they were openly pulicized by the Greek Parliament and the Greek press. Palmerston accused Poniropoulos of deliberately holding money back which was available in the Public Treasury to pay the interest to the Powers. He stated that Great Britain paid the Rothchild Bank on behalf of Greece 196,933 pounds sterling from March 1843 until March 1847 because the Greek government systematically and willfully chose to violate the terms of the 1832 Treaty. He warned that his government would not continue to tolerate the present situation but if Greece resumed regular payments on the interest Britain would not force the Greek kingdom to submit all the arrears on the interest and sinking fund due to her. The British Foreign Secretary instructed Lyons to inform Kolettes that Greece had to pay immediately the amount of 23,570.17 pounds sterling to the Rothchild Bank for the March 1847 instalment. Palmerston asked Lyons to submit the following message to the Cabinet at Athens.

> You will at the same time declare plainly to the Greek government that it must itself make provisions for the future instalments of the interest and sinking fund on the British portion of the loan, and you will request Mr. Coletti to state what arrangement he proposes to make for the gradual repayment of the remaining part of the sum which Great Britain has thus unduly been called upon to advance on account of the government of Greece.[95]

The reasons behind Palmerson's desire to put financial pressure on Greece were purely political but he also resented the Kolettes administration for deceiving him about Greek intentions to dissolve the foreign debt.

Palmerston knew that in 1845 the Greek Treasury had a surplus of 700,000 drachmas which the Parliament voted in February 1847 to alocate to Britain and Russia for the interest and sinking fund.[96] The Cabinet, that is, Kolettes, chose to hold that money in Greece and did not send it to its intended destination.

After Lyons sent a copy of Palmerston's dispatch (no. 33, 6 April 1847) to Kolettes the Foreign Office ordered the British fleet at Malta to tour the Greek waters. Palmerston hoped that a naval display would convince Otho and his Prime Minister to yield to Britain's political demands.[97] Palmerston's display of force in Greece alarmed France who appealed to Austria and Russia to use their concerted influence in London to prevent British threats against Greece.[98] On 8 July 1847 Lyons wrote to the Greek Foreign Ministry that Palmerston had renewed his demand for payment on the loan and that:

> Her Majesty's government hope and trust that it will be complied with without any further delay, and without its being

necessary for her Majesty's government to resort to any other
means than friendly representation in order to obtain satis-
factory results.[99]

The officials in Athens were terrified by such warnings and apparent
signs of aggression by Britain. They were desperate to satisfy Palmerston's
demands before he adopted any drastic measures against the Protectorate.
In this crisis Greece was saved by a Genevan philhellene banker, Jean
Gabriel Eynard, who offered Greece a short term loan. Eynard wrote a
very sympathetic letter to Kolettes in which he expressed his concern
with Greek financial difficulties and the nation's inability to liquidate
her foreign debt.[100] He offered 500,000 francs to cover the six-month
British instalment for March 1847.[101] The Hellenic government added to
this sum 95,164.15 francs to equal the amount paid by Great Britain to
the Rothchild Bank in March.

Palmerston was not satisfied with just one payment on the interest
and sinking fund and after he received it he demanded that Greece should
pay all the arrears which totalled 196,933 pounds sterling.[102] Before he
received the instalment payment for March 1847 he ascertained that
Britain would not ask Greece for the arrears due on the interest but that
the Cabinet in Athens should make an effort to keep up with future
payments. He realized, however, that his pressure tactics against Greece
worked and that France was unable to gain sufficient diplomatic pressure
against Britain. He decided therefore to continue his financial pressure
tactics against the Protectorate so that King Otho would be forced to
ultimately accept "British" party politicians in the government. This was
the end result which Palmerston wanted to achieve. By using the excuse
of the Greek foreign debt he believed that the king would ultimately
bend to British wishes.

The Foreign Office asked Kolettes to devise a plan on how his government proposed to liquidate the arrears due to the Powers. In January
1847 the Greek Prime Minister composed such a plan in which he proposed that Greece wanted to dissolve the arrears progressively until 1860
and thereafter resume instalment charges in their entirety.[103] Palmerston
denounced this plan as vague which did not indicate any systematic
manner in which the interest and sinking fund or the arrears could be met
in the future.[104] The British government made it clear to the officials in

Athens that it did not want to compromise on the issue of the arrears, and would therefore not accept any Greek proposals on this matter which were intended to avoid payment of the arrears. Lyons shifted the issue from the arrears to the September instalment and demanded prompt action by the Kolettes Cabinet.[105]

In August Palmerston issued a demand to Greece which required that, "one third of the first produce of the whole revenue of Greece, from whatever source arising, shall be applied to pay the interest and sinking fund of that part of the Greek loan which has been guaranteed by England."[106] The Foreign Secretary also reminded the Hellenic government of its obligations to redeem the bondholders of 1824 and 1825 loans and once again Palmerston reiterated his stance that Great Britain would not compromise on these issues with the Kolettes administration.[107] Palmerstonian diplomacy in Greece rapidly became hostile and uncompromising not because Great Britain needed the few pounds which Greece owed her but because the Greek King and his Prime Minister entertained an anti-Turkish foreign policy which interfered with Palmerston's Near Eastern foreign policy and because the Kolettes administration had so effectively used France to minimize British influence in Greece.[108]

In September 1847 Greece defaulted again the instalment payments to the Powers. The British Legation informed the Greek Minister of Foreign Affairs that England did not intend to issue any future payments to the Rothchild Bank on the interest and sinking fund on the Greek government's behalf.[109] Kolettes died in September and left the country with an enormous foreign debt. While he was Prime Minister for three years he made no efforts to reduce the nation's foreign debt, or to reduce Anglo-Greek tensions. The following table was designed by the Financial Commission of 1857-1859 and it reveals the state of the Greek foreign debt six months before Kolettes' death.

Puissances	Nobre des obligations	Capital Nominal a[110]
	émises au 1er Mars 1847	1,024 francs
France	16,992 10/12 francs	17,400,661.34 francs
Grande		
Bretagne	19,373 10/12 francs	19,838,805.33 francs
Russie	19,530 10/12 francs	19,999,573.33 francs
Total	55,897 6/12 francs	57,239,040.00 francs

Puissances	Arrerages a 6%	Chiffre des avances au 1 er
		Mars 1847
France	1,044,039.68 francs	7,159,120.06 francs
Grande		
Bretagne	1,190,328.32 francs	5,076,708.87 francs
Russie	1,199,974.40 francs	5,120,555.07 francs
Total	3,434,342.40 francs	17,356,384.00 francs

The British believed that Kolettes' death marked the end of French dominant influence in Greece. Palmerston wanted the end of Francophilism in Athens and the restoration of British influence in the Hellenic government.[111] He tried to achieve this goal but Otho who was more anti-British than Kolettes refused to yield to Palmerson's pressures and would not appoint a pro-British Cabinet. After Kolettes died the Greek monarch decided to take the government into his own hands without violating the Constitution. From September 1847 until May 1854 Otho appointed a number of puppet Prime Ministers who were loyal to him and not to their party or any foreign government as was Kolettes. The various Ministries which he appointed did not have any politicians from the "English" party but were made up by "French" and "Russian" party politicians who owed their allegiance to Otho and carried out his domestic and foreign policies.[112] The King and his puppet Cabinets continued the expansionist foreign policy which Kolettes initiated. Otho; also followed Kolettes' example of antagonizing the British and neglecting to liquidate the nation's foreign debt.

Since the Greek Monarch refused to compromise with the Foreign Office on the issue of appointing a pro-British Cabinet in Athens, Palmerston refused to compromise with Otho on the issue of the Greek foreign debt. When the new Greek Ministry took power in September[113] the British Legation wanted to be certain that the new Foreign Ministry understood Britain's position on the Greek foreign debt. Lyons wrote to G. Glarakes, the Foreign Minister, that Greece had not taken any measures to pay the interest and sinking fund charges due on 1 September 1847.[114] The British representative also wished to clarify his government's position to Glarakes on the Kolettes proposal of August 1847. According to the former Prime Minister's plan "the Greek government

proposes to arrive gradually and after thirteen years at the payment of
the whole amount of the interest and sinking fund of the loan . . . ."[115]
This was the same proposal as that of January 1847 but the Foreign
Office had repeatedly rejected any compromise on the Greek foreign
debt.

Palmerston instructed Lyons in October to inform Glarakes that the
Greek State should yield the first produce of the public revenue to the
payment of the interest and sinking fund. The Greek government's practice in regards to this matter was to apply the surplus to the foreign debt,
and the first produce to the service of the State. Since there was hardly
any revenue surplus the Greek foreign debt kept rising. Palmerston accused Greece of violating the Treaty of 1832, Article XII, because it
carried out a policy by which it did not dedicate the first produce of
the country's revenues to the instalment payments. Furthermore, the
British Foreign Secretary accused the Greek government of financial
mismanagement and added that England could not be burdened with
the Greek debts.[116] As far as the Kolettes proposal concerning the use
of National Lands as a possible source of public revenue, Palmerston
argued that it was unacceptable to Great Britain because the National
Estates were mortgaged to the British bondholders and could not be
alienated.[117]

Inspite of Britain's warnings and demands to Greece concerning the
consequences of the latter's neglect to meet her financial obligations
toward the Powers the Cabinet at Athens ignored Palmerston's and Lyon's
requests to pay the instalment of September 1847. In November Lyons
reiterated his government's position to Glarakes and reminded the Greek
Foreign Minister that the Hellenic State should give its immediate attention to the issue of the September instalment.[118] The Greek Public Treasury lacked any surplus revenues to apply towards the annual charges
on the loan, but the Cabinet realized that it somehow had to pay Britian
for the advance she made on behalf of Greece in September. Since the
Public Treasury could not afford to remit the September instalment
in cash the Hellenic government offered payment in the form of Greek
National Bank shares. The Foreign Office instructed Lyons not to accept
any other form of payment which the Greeks offered except that which
Britain used to pay the Rothschild Bank.[119]

The British Legation's response to Glarakes aggravated Greek officials
in Athens for they believed that while the administration tried to cooperate

with British demands for payment of the instalments, the Foreign Office refused any such cooperation and compromise on its part. Glarakes wrote to Lyons that Greece acted in good faith by offering Britain the National Bank shares. He added that the King's government had every intention to repay its foreign debt. The Greek Foreign Minister expressed his government's disappointment with England's uncompromising position concerning the form of payment which Greece offered, and he stated that it was his conviction that British officials misunderstood and did not take seriously the National Bank shares.[120]

The administration in Athens did not offer England an alternative form of payment in 1847 for the interest and sinking fund. At the end of that year Greek defered instalment payments to Great Britain alone amounted to 200,000 pounds sterling.[121] This astronomical figure reflected Otho's inability to direct his government in devising a systematic financial plan in order to liquidate the mounting foreign debt. The Greek monarch was not concerned with the country's foreign debt and its political implications while Kolettes was in power because Guizot patronized the Prime Minister. French foreign policy however after Kolettes' death changed because Otho took power into his own hands from all three parties. Glarakes was concerned with the changing French foreign policy in Greece and also with Russia's cold policy toward Greece. In February 1848 he wrote to the Russian and French Legations in Athens to assure them that his government intended to place at the Powers' disposition the sum of 600,000 drachmas for the instalment of 1 March 1848.[122] He added that Greece made great efforts to dissolve her foreign debt, but Great Britain antagonized the Protectorate and put financial pressures on it by demanding full payment of the arrears due on the charges of the loan.[123] The Greek foreign minister hoped to use the French and Russian legations as a balance to diminish British financial pressures in Athens, but neither the Russian nor the French governments committed themselves to Glarakes.

In February 1848 the Greek Ministry of Finance allocated 572,390.40 francs to the Powers for the interest and sinking fund due in March of that year. England received 198,388.60, Russia 199,995.73 and France 174,066.61.[124] The French and the Russian governments received the Greek payments and expressed some satisfaction and renewed optimism about the Greek government's financial obligations. The British Legation, however, was not satisfied with just one payment and Lyons wrote to

Glarakes that his government demanded that Greece should pay all the defered instalments since 1843.[125] Furthermore the British Chargá d' Affaires requested that in the future the Hellenic State should make all payments on its debt on their due dates and also make them payable directly to the Rothschild Bank. He advised Greek officials that if they eliminated financial abuses and corruption in their government, Greece would not encounter any difficulties in dissolving her foreign debt and meeting instalment payments on their due dates.[126]

Greek officials were increasingly alarmed with Britain's hostile position toward Greece. As far as many Greeks were concerned, Palmerston antagonized the government in Athens deliberately for he did not express any tolerance, gratitude or optimism as did the other two guaranteeing governments after Greece made a promise to pay the March instalment.[127] Palmerston had political reasons for pursuing an antagonistic policy in Greece and that was the reason that he did not have either French or Russian support for his pursuant demands to the Cabinet in Athens for full payment of the arrears.

When the European Revolution of 1848 broke out, Greece was also affected by sporadic antimonarchical revolts which forced the cabinet's fall.[128] The King appointed a Francophile Prime Minister, G. Koundouriotes, to form a new cabinet.[129] Lyons attempted to persuade Otho to accept the Anglophile, A. Mavrokordatos as the new prime minister, but the King refused because Mavrokordatos did not entertain an expansionist foreign policy and that was the Court's primary issue of importance.[130] Palmerston was still determined to have a pro-British cabinet in Athens so in June he sent Stratford Canning, ambassador in Constantinople, to Athens. Canning's mission was to persuade Otho to yield to Palmerston's wishes. The result of the ambassador's mission was a failure to the degree that Otho persuaded Canning that Lyons was the cause of Anglo-Greek tensions.[131]

After he failed to secure an anglophile cabinet in Athens, Palmerston declared that he would never approve a government in Greece unless its leader was from the "English" party.[132] The Foreign Office decided to use financial pressure, the only effective weapon at its disposal, against Greece and King Otho. In April 1848, Palmerston instructed Lyons to request from the Greek foreign minister, "that the reminder (of the deferred payments due to Britain) shall be paid without delay."[133] Greece did not respond to that demand for a variety of reasons. In 1848 Otho was forced to dismiss two unpopular cabinets, because social revolts spread throughout Greece and presented a threat to the monarchy. Greek military expenditure therefore increased for security reasons. In September Greece failed again to discharge the instalments due to the Powers. France and Russia did not demand any explanations for the default but Palmerston was eager to find Greece in such a vulnerable position and requested the administration at Athens to design a new plan which outlined the manner that Greece proposed to liquidate the arrears due to the Powers.[134] The Hellenic State did not design a plan to Palmerston's satisfaction and the matter remained unresolved.

During the Kolettes administration Greece had not only neglected the debt owed to the Powers but also the Bavarian loan. The Greek government did not make any payments to King Ludwig's government since 1843 but Otho's father was much more tolerant with Greece than was Palmerston. One of the reasons that the cabinet failed to dissolve the Bavarian debt was due to pressure from the foreign office. In March 1838, Palmerston demanded that Greece should not use any revenues to pay the Bavarian loan[135] because the guaranteed loan of 1832 had priority. In December 1848, King Ludwig's government asked the Greek foreign minister to take measures to discharge the debt owed to Bavaria.[136] Bavarian officials expressed sympathy for Otho's financial, political and diplomatic difficulties, but they nevertheless demanded that the administration in Athens should resolve the financial differences between Bavaria and Greece. Konstantinos Kolokotrones, the Greek foreign minister, assured King Ludwig's government that the cabinet gave serious consideration to the Bavarian loan and devised a proposal to liquidate the debt before consideration.[137] Bavaria did not make any more serious demands for the payment for the 1835 loan until 1852 and Greece was free to redirect her attention to the more serious matter of the guaranteed loan.

The Great Powers, like Bavaria, did not make any serious demands to Greece for payment of the charges on the guaranteed loan after 1849 until the opening of the Holy Places question. The reason that the Foreign Office avoided the issue of the Greek foreign debt from 1849 until 1851 was due to Palmerston's engineering of certain greivances involving the interests of English citizens who resided in Greece and the Ionian Islands against the Hellenic State. The grievances of British citizens against Greece concerned the settlement of financial matters between private citizens and the Greek government. Palmerston used these issues against Greece since financial pressures against the administration had not produced major results to Britain's satisfaction. The administration in Athens knew Palmerston's political motives behind his concern for financial settlement for the British citizens and refused to abide by his wishes.[138] The State argued that if British subjects had any legal grievances against Greece or against subjects of the kingdom they should settled them in the courts, not through the foreign office.[139] Palmerston who antagonized Greece for thirteen years ordered Admiral Parker to blockade the Pireaus port in January 1850.[140] The blockade created a major diplomatic rupture between England and the European community and after international and even British domestic pressure to remove the blockade in Greece, Palmerston cooperated.[141]

The British blockade diverted Britain's and the Power's attention from the Greek guaranteed loan. But the economic and political damage inflicted upon Greece as a result of the British blockade was enormous and it only excellerated and increased anti-British sentiments in Greece.[142]

C.   Anglo-French Concerted Policy in Greece, 1852-1854

From 1850 until 1857, the year that the Great Powers established a Financial Commission in Athens to examine Greek finances, Otho's foreign policy was pro-Russian. A number of factors contributed to this change of policy[143] but most important of all was King Otho's and Tsar Nicholas' agreement on their Near Eastern foreign policy. Both wanted to expand territorially at Turkey's expense. Even though the Tsar did not wish Greece to expand territorially to the north, he did want her as an ally due to her strategic location.

From the beginning of the Holy Places question, the Greek population sided with Otho and Russia against the Sublime Porte and France.[144] When diplomatic hostilities ruptured between the Sublime Porte and the Tsar's government, the Greek Court sided with Russia against the Western powers.[145] In view of Otho's pro-Russian and anti-Turkish foreign policy before the Crimean War the Western Powers were forced to defend their Near Eastern interests which Russia and Greece threatened. In 1852 France and England started concerted efforts to neutralize Greece in the Russo-Turkish diplomatic dispute. In January Eduard Thouvennel, French ambassador in Constantinople, who unlike Palmerston, was very sympathetic to Greece and especially to Otho until the beginning of the Holy Places question, informed Alexander Mavrokordatos, Greek representative in Paris, that the French government wanted a quick settlement of Franco-Greek financial matters. Thouvennel advised Mavrokordatos that if the Hellenic government could not apply the entire amount on the arrears owed to France, the officials in Athens should at least make an effort to pay the highest possible sums.[146] Mavrokordatos took the liberty of replying to Thouvennel without first consulting with the administration in Athens. He assured the French ambassador that Greece could afford to submit 1,278,491 drachmas to each Power for the charges on the loan.[147]

Mavrokordatos based this figure on budget revenues and not actual receipts which in Greece were always considerably lower than the government estimates, due to arrears mismanagement and corruption. The Greek foreign minister, A. Paicos, consulted with the Ministry of Finance to verify his suspicion that the Public Treasury could not possibly withstand such high payments to the Powers as Mavrokordatos suggested to Thouvennel, D. Christides, the Minister of Finance, confirmed Paicos' suspicions, and criticized Mavrokordatos for speculating on matters on which he had no knowledge. Christides explained to Paicos that the actual revenues were always lower than the budget estimates. The reason for this, the minister maintained, was not due to mismanagement or corruption as the British charged, but due to the arrears which were not collected, and of course to the unpredictability of the national economy itself.

The government revenue estimates in 1851 for Custom Duties were 3,765,000 drachmas, Christides pointed out, but the actual receipts were only 2,900,000 drachmas.[148] The Minister of Finance added that the nation's revenues had suffered severely in the past two years as a result of reductions in agricultural production. In 1851 the budget estimate for receipts stemming from agricultural produce were eleven million drachmas but the Public Treasury collected only seven million. Given the country's economic realities and the government's weak finances, the Minister concluded that it was impossible for Greece to meet the Powers' demands on the foreign debt.[149]

In the beginning of 1852 Bavaria renewed her demands to Greece for the interest and sinking fund charges. The Bavarian minister at Athens, Baron Perglos, wrote to Paicos that King Ludwig's government wanted Greek officials to give their attention to the arrears due on the instalments of the Bavarian loan.[150] Perglos maintained that the Greek government had assured him on two previous occasions, 20 March 1849, and 4 December 1848, that it would fulfill the sacred Treaty between Bavaria and Greece in regards to the loan. The Bavarian minister wanted Paicos' reassurance that the cabinet in Athens would not violate the Treaty of 1835 between the two friendly nations and that it would fulfill the terms of the contracted loan.[151]

Although Perglos and his government were not in the position to use diplomatic pressure on Greece, nor were they willing to force the latter into a settlement of the debt, the Greek debt was increasing through they years and Otho made no efforts to reduce it. He did not only neglect to discharge the debt due to the Powers and to the British bondholders but he also disregarded the debt to his father. Few Greek politicians and bureaucrats foresaw the consequences of Otho's financial irresponsibility to the Powers but no one expected the King to take any action on this matter. According to the Minister of Finance the government could only afford an annual sum of 400,000 drachmas for the interest on the guaranteed loan. The guaranteeing governments, however, paid an annual sum on the Hellenic government's behalf of 3,835,473.58 drachmas, or 1,278,491.19 francs for each Power, to the Rothschild Bank.[152]

The British Legation refused to believe that Greece could even afford to allocate the minimal sum of 400,000 drachmas to the Powers. The British representative at Athens questioned Christides' integrity, and his statements concerning the state of the Greek economy and the Public Treasury as the following dispatch revealed. The author of the dispatch was Sir Thomas Wyse[153] who replaced Lyons as minister at Athens, but shared Lyons' contempt for Otho and his suspicions about the Greek government. He wrote to the Foreign Office:

The receipts for the year 1853 are calculated (exclusive of the advances of the Three Powers drachmas 3,835,473.58) at 17,701,966 drachmas and this is stated to surplus the amount given in the budget of 1852 by 454,000 drachmas. But it is admitted to suffer a considerable dimunition inthe collection. The expenditure (exclusive of the payment of Interest and Sinking fund on the loan equivalent to the advances of the Three Powers) makes a total of 15,572,608 drachmas and 35 lepta. This gives according to Mr. Chrestides a surplus of about 50,000 of receipts over expenditures. This in itself is a miserable balance but what is worse is that it is unreal. The annual interest on the loan remains unpaid and is carried over in this as in preceeding years, largely to raise the permanent debt of the country. It is true indeed that 400,000 drachmas to the Three Powers heads as by Treaty bound the estimates of expenditures, but a similar sum in similar form was not put forward in last year's budget but was either not forthcoming or misapplied to other purposes. . . . The real result then is this, that not only there is no surplus, but a heavy deficit (supposing obligations to be insisted on) of 3,835,473.58 with Receipts of at most 17,000,000 drachmas to met it.[154]

Unfortunately, Wyse's observations on Greek finances before the Crimean War were accurate.

In spite of Christides' efforts to conceal the real state of the Public Treasury, the British government knew that the Greek government's promises to pay the nation's foreign debt could not possibly materialize. Even though the administration in Athens had devised a number of proposals which dealt with the liquidation of the foreign debt, the only real weapon left for Otho to counterbalance Western European financial pressures on Greece, was diplomacy. As long as the King and the cabinet had the support of at least one of the three Powers the other two were forced to be lenient towards the Protectorate.

After 1850 King Otho supported Russian foreign policy in the Near East and the Tsar returned the favor in 1853. When France and Great Britain cooperated in their efforts to neutralize the Russian influence in Greece by demanding payment on the instalment and the arrears of the 1832 loan, Russia did not cooperate. The government in St. Petersburg announced at the beginning of 1853 that Tsar Nicholas did not wish to contribute to Greek economic and financial discomfort by accepting the 400,000 drachmas instalment payments which the cabinet in Athens offered. The Russian government granted Greece a four-year grace period on the annual instalments. Christides politely declined to accept the Russian generosity and stated that his government had but the best intentions concerning the country's financial obligations to the Powers.[155] The Greek minister of finance, however, was unable to substantiate his claims with cash payments. The Tsar allowed the matter to stand as long of course as Greek foreign policy served Russian interests in the Near East.

The Western Powers believed that the reasons for the Greek Public Treasury's weaknesses were due to corruption in the administration, Christides' incompetence as a finance minister and Otho's extravagant spending. The French Legation blamed mostly the minister of finance for the country's poor state of finances and in October Forth-Rouen, the French representative in Athens, convinced Otho to dismiss Christides from office. The reason for Christides' dismissal was not due to his incompetence as a finance minister but to his political affiliation with the "Russian" party.[156] Wyse and Forth-Rouen knew that Christides' resignation would not improve the nation's finances nor would it make any difference on Otho's attitude toward the Western Powers. They wanted him eliminated, however, from a cabinet which was dominated by "Russian" party politicians who sympathized with the Tsar's anti-Turkish policy and opposed the Western Powers.

The king appointed K. Provelgios as the new minister of finance, a member of the "French" party. Two days after Provelgios took office the Greek Parliament (Chamber of Deputies) passed a bill to contract a loan for five million drachmas.[157] The rate of interest was six percent and as security for the loan the Government offered the creditors one thousand shares in the National Bank of Greece amounting to 1,200,000 drachmas, as well as other floating public revenues. The Government used portions of the National Property as mortgage for the loan but the Cabinet did not make an official announcement that Greece negotiated a loan and it did not name the lending institution.[158] According to newspaper reports, the lenders were shareholders of the National Bank of Greece. Wyse who was informed by intelligence sources concerning the Government's loan negotiations wrote to the Foreign Office:

> The Bank has declared itself ready to make the loan required
> at the rate indicated, so as to open a current account with the

government, paying its drafts up to the amount stated, in pro-
portion as it received securities to meet it, and is willing to consider such, the shares offered at present of the Bank, the contract
for five years rental of the emery mines of Naxos and the commercial bills due to the Treasury from the merchants of the ports
of Syra and Piraeus.[159]

According to the loan's Articles of Agreement the Government consented
to pay six percent interest until the end of 1858 and at the beginning of
1859 one percent sinking fund charge would be added. The loan was
divided into five thousand shares at one thousand drachmas each.[160]

According to the Cabinet the purpose of the proposed loan was the
establishment of more Greek embassies around the world in order to
promote the nation's interests.[161] Since the five million drachmas was
not designed to liquidate the country's foreign debt the Great Powers
opposed the loan. Wyse asked the Russian and French representatives
to join him in submitting a formal protect against the loan to the Hellenic
government. The British charge d'affairs insisted that such action was
necessary in order to prove to King Otho and to the cabinet in Athens
the Powers' solidarity and opposition to the proposed loan. Persiany,
however, refused to go along with Wyse's proposal. He stated that the
Tsar's government had already granted a four-year grace period to Greece
on the annual instalments due to Russia and could not protest against
the porposed loan after it promised to be lenient toward the King's financial affairs.[162] Forth-Rouen maintained that he could not endorse
Wyse's proposal unless Persiany fully cooperated with Wyse. The French
and Russian charge d'affaires did not cooperate with Wyse for political
reasons even though they both objected to the loan and its purpose.
Persiany and Forth-Rouen did not want to offend Otho's government
because the cabinet was composed of members who belonged to the
"French" and "Russian" parties.

Wyse, however, had every reason to protest. He wrote to Paicos that
Greece violated the Treaty of 1832 by proposing to raise a loan secretly
from the Powers. He maintained that the Hellenic government should
have contracted the guaranteeing governments before it contemplated
any loan. Paicos replied that the Loan of 1832 "made by the Three
Powers ought to have been a gift and not a loan, and he (Paicos) looked
upon its redemption as a very remote and problematical contigency."[163]

The Greek foreign minister's reply shocked Wyse, but the British representative was shocked even more after Greek newspaper reports revealed the real purpose of the loan. Originally the government justified the loan by claiming that it needed to expand its diplomatic service. According to the press reports, however, the loan was intended to place Greece in a financially advantageous position in case of a Russo-Turkish war.[164]

When Forth-Rouen read the press reports he changed his attitude about the Greek government. Originally, the French representative withheld from Anglo-French concerted action against Greece because he believed such action would have caused Otho to replace the few pro-French politicians in the cabinet with pro-Russian ones.[165] This was a gross political miscalculation on Forth-Rouen's part because the Cabinet was predominately "Russian" and even the "French" party members in the government sympathized with Otho's irredentist foreign policy.

A few days after Wyse requested Forth-Rouen's cooperation to formally protest against the Greek proposed loan, the French charge d'affaires complied with the British Legation's request.[166] Paicos was then left with the Russian Legation's support only and he was forced to respond to Anglo-French protestations. He explained to Wyse and Rouen that the loan was necessary to aid the weak Greek finances which had suffered severe setbacks as a result of considerable agricultural setbacks since 1849. Furthermore, the foreign minister stated that a portion of the proposed loan would have been used to dissolve the country's foreign debt.[167] Paicos sent copies of his dispatch concerning his government's official position on the loan's destination to the Greek embassies in London, Paris and St. Petersburg. The foreign minister instructed the Greek ambassadors to personally give an account of the true reasons for the contemplated loan to the foreign ministers of the guaranteeing governments. Paicos resorted to such action because he believed that the Powers' ministers in Athens were prejudiced by the press reports concerning the loan's purpose and could not possibily therefore provide an "objective" account to the respective governments. Count Nesselrode and Drouyn de Lhuys, foreign ministers of Russia and France respectively, received Paicos' dispatch with moderate reaction.[168] Lord Clarendon, the British foreign secretary, refused to accept the Paicos' explanation and instrcted Lyons to inform the government in Athens of Britain's official position.[169]

Paicos charged that the Foreign Office's reluctance to accept his explanations concerning the loan was due to Wyse's misinterpretation of the facts to Lord Clarendon.[170] Wyse responded that as Minister of Britain he was obliged to act according to the Treaty of 1832 (Article XII paragraph six) and he did exactly that without exceeding his authority or have ulterior motives.[171] Before the controversy involving Wyse and Paicos went any further, the Greek government announced that there were no lenders for the five million drachmas loan and Anglo-Greek tensions eased for a short period.[172] British and to a lesser extent French attempts to prevent Greece from raising a loan in 1853 were a clear indication that the Powers used the Treaty of 1832 to justify their intervention in Greek internal affairs. Britain and to a lesser extent France intervened in Greek financial affairs and used pressure tactics in Greece in order to direct that government's foreign policy. This was a clear violation of the 1832 treaty and more important a violation of the Greek nation's sovereignty.

The Western Powers flirted with direct intervention in Greek affairs ever since the kingdom was created. Finally a chain of events in 1854 accounted for a Franco-British occupation of Greece. During the first five months of 1854, Greece engaged in an undeclared war against the Ottoman empire. The Greeks contemplated such a conflict ever since the Kolettes administration and the Russo-Turkish diplomatic hostilities which resulted in a war in 1854 gave Greece the opportunity to strike the Turkish provinces of Thessaly, Epirus and Chalcidice.[173]

In February 1854 the French government became increasinly concerned with Greek Russophilism and rising anti-Turkish sentiments among Greeks. Forth-Rouen and Wyse started to cooperate in an attempt to diminish Russophilism in the administration by using financial pressure against the Protectorate. The French Charge d'Affaires informed Paicos that the instalment on the interest and sinking fund was due and that France wished the government in Athens to give this matter its utmost consideration. Forth-Rouen charged that Greece for too long had neglected this issue and the French foreign minister insisted on the Greek government's strict observance of her financial obligation toward the Powers.[174] Wyse followed his French colleague's footsteps to reiterate the British stand on this matter. He wrote to Paicos that the Greek Chamber of Deputies authorized the cabinet to raise a loan in 1853 in violation of the 1832 Treaty, but that same body of officials did not take any action to dissolve the Greek foreign debt. He continued, "the first revenues of the Greek State, as well as the resources of the land, should be devoted, before anything else to the payment of the interest and sinking fund of the guaranteed loan by the Powers."[175] Wyse reminded the Greek foreign minister that the Foreign Office expected Greece to strictly observe the Article of the Treaty of 1832 in regards to repayment of the loan.

The insurrection in Thessaly and Epirus accelerated in the spring of 1854 and Turkey was faced with the danger of fighting a two front war, one in the southwest against Greece and the other in the northeast against Russia. The Western Powers who wished to prevent such a course of events stiffened their pressure on Greece. The British Legation demanded satisfaction from the Greek Minister of Finance for the bondholer's claims of 1824 and 1825. Wyse claimed that the Greek government had paid no interest to the bondholders ever since Otho became king and demanded immediate payment without further delays.[176] On 5 April Provelgios, the finance minister, informed Paicos that the Allied Powers insisted that payments on the foreign debt should be on time henceforth for both France and England had lost their patience with the officials at Athens.[177]

Paicos once again attempted to convince Forth-Rouen and Wyse that the reasons for the Greek default were due to the deplorable economic conditions of the nation and to the weak Public Treasury. He reminded the British and French representatives that the Treasury suffered deficits when the government tried to raise a loan in 1853 and that the purpose of that loan was to cover the 1854 deficit. He further stated that France and Great Britain knew that the Greek Treasury suffered deficits and her economy was weak but both Powers tried to obstruct the cabinet's efforts to raise a loan while at the same time they demanded payment on the annual instalment charges.[178] Wyse responded that France and England had always acted in the best interests of Greece even though the administration in Athens antagonized the Western Powers and upset their Near Eastern policy. Once again the British minister reminded Paicos that the Foreign Office insisted on Greece's observance of the Treaty of 1832.[179]

Forth-Rouen and Wyse agreed with the Greek Foreign Minister that his country's economy and finances were indeed in a chaotic state, and they informed their governments of the true financial and economic situation in Greece. Wyse reported to the Foreign Office that Greek agricultural production steadily decreased since 1849 and that there was indeed little hope according to the Greek Foreign Minister that the nation would be in the position to repay her foreign debt for several years. Wyse added that in his opinion the vast Greek bureaucracy absorbed much of the country's revenues.[180] During this period in which the Allied Powers asked Greece to discharge her financial obligations toward them the King secretly supported the Greek-Turkish war in the Turkish provinces adjacent to Greece. The Western Powers felt that while Greece suffered economically and the Treasury was empty, Otho and his cabinet found sufficient funds to support an insurrection against Turkey. From the Allied Power's viewpoint Otho supported Russian policy in the Near East and opposed the Western Powers[181] so he had to be stopped.

Since financial pressure did not discourage Greece from carrying out their militaristic adventure in the spring of 1854, the Allied Powers, after warning Greece several times, occupied the country. On 26 May 1854, French troops entered the Pireaus Port after Otho refused to stop the insurrection in the Provinces. The occupation, as Wyse justified it, was an attempt to neutralize Greece in the Russo-Turkish conflict and to aid the Greek nation "in every effort to maintain a peaceable and friendly attitude towards their neighbors, to service their commerce, to develop their industry, to extend in every manner their civilization."[182] The British occupied a free nation against its will because it obstructed their foreign policy and they justified their occupation so brilliantly that one wonders why did they not occupy Greece earlier and deliver that backward nation from chaos to civilization.

After the occupation King Otho was forced by the Allied Powers to replace the Russophile administration[183] with a pro-British and pro-French cabinet headed by the anglophile A. Mavrokordatos. The new prime minister, like his predecessor found the Greek economy and finances extremly weak. The French government asked Mavrokordatos after he took power to devise a proposal which outlined the program which he would adopt as prime minister to deal effectively with the liquidation of the Greek foreign debt.[184]

Mavrokordatos asked the Allied Powers to be patient and lenient toward Greece due to the nation's financial status in 1854. In September he informed the Powers' Legations at Athens that Greece could not meet the instalment payment due that month. The prime minister blamed his cabinet's inability to discharge the instalment, on the reduction of the country's agricultural output, the cholera that broke out in Athens, the decrease in commerce activity and other financial and economic consequences which resulted from the Allied occupation.[185] The Russian Legation's response to Mavrokordatos' statement was as expected quite moderate. Persiany simply stated that he would inform his government in St. Petersburg about the current Greek financial condition but he reassured Mavrokordatos that Russia had accorded Greece a four-year grace period on all annual instalments due to the Tsar's government.[186] Forth-Rouen was also sympathetic to the Prime Minister who took power in the midst of a crisis and who inherited an emply Public Treasury and economic stagnation.[187] Drouyn de Lhuys was also kind to Mavrokordatos and like Forth-Rouen admitted that the prime minister inherited the country's current problems from a previous irresponsible administration.[188]

For the first time since Count Armansperg's fall, the head of the government in Athens was an anglophile. The Foreign Office therefore was lenient towards Mavrokordatos upon his announcement of the September default. Lord Clarendon did insist, however, that "for the honour of the Greek Government and the establishment of its credit, it is much to be desired that bonafide efforts should be made for the regular payment of the interest."[189] Wyse sent a copy of this message to the prime minister and used the opportunity to severely criticize Mavrokordatos's predecessors in the government. He attacked the numerous attempts by previous ministers of finance to avoid payments on the annual interest and sinking fund. The British minister insisted that past administrations deliberately ignored the country's foreign debt and refused to deal with it as though it never existed. He charged that previous finance ministers were incompetent, negligent, guilty of public betrayal and they had disregarded their duties as government officials.[190]

There is no doubt in the light of the existing archival documentation that Wyse was correct in his assessment of the Greek administration under King Otho. His motives, however, are questionable. He never cared about the state of Greek finances or about Greek economic progress or about government corruption. Wyse and his government were only interested in using Greece as their satelite country, exploiting it financially and politically. The history of Anglo-Greek relations from 1833 until the Franco-British occupation was one of constant attempts by the Foreign Office to gain political influence in the administration at Athens.

CHAPTER III

THE NATIONAL ESTATES ISSUE

A. *Agricultural Progress During Otho's Reign and the National Estates*

The Public Treasury contained 60 pounds sterling when Prince Otho arrived at Nauplion in 1833.[1] The War of Independence and the incompetent insurgent governments were responsible for the dormant Greek economy. Greece was an agricultural nation so naturally during the first years of Othonian rule the majority of the public revenues derived from the agrarian economic sector. The table below indicates the government's dependence on agriculture for its income.

Year	Land Tax	Total Revenue[2]
1833	4,219,275	7,042,653
1834	5,650,705	9,455,410
1835	8,749,407	12,383,955
1836	8,885,000	12,842,445
1837	8,650,000	31,933,980

Inspite of the agrarian sector's enormous contributions to the Public Treasury, the Greek government did not aid that economic sector and it even contributed to its regress.

During his reign Otho retained the archaic tax structure in Greece which had its origin the feudal Ottoman empire. As a result of the Turkish feudal agrarian tax system which Greece adoped, many small farmers were reduced to semi-serfdom. According to that tax system the landowner was not taxed on the quantity of his land, but on the gross annual produce of his farm. The farmer yielded ten percent of his gross produce to the government before he even had the opportunity to balance his budget.[3] The tax collectors were large landowners who abused the tax-system and extorted a great deal more from the farmers and returned less than they took to the State. One contemporary scholar characterized the effects of this archaic tax structure as follows:

> By this oriental system of taxation the whole agricultural produce
> of the country is in the hands of the Farmer (large landowner).
> So that the cultivator of the soil is converted into the serf of
> the Farmer, or collector of the tax, for several months.[4]

In the early 1830s one half million, of a total population of seven hundred thousand were classified as agricultural laborers or farmers.[5] Less than two hundred thousand owned land and they only averaged twenty strem-mata per family. The rest of the population was landless.

The ministry of finance which the Bavarians established in Greece in April 1834 did not take any measures to improve the status of the agrarian population even though it was within its means to do so.[6] The total amount of arable land during the Othonian era was 2,003,000 hectares; 800,000 hectares belong to the government, but only 500,000 hectares out of the total arable land was under cultivation during Otho's reign, and only 136,800 hectares from the National arable land was ever culti-vated. Over one and a half million hectares of arable land laid fallow.[7] Even so agricultural production steadily increased from thirty million drachmas in 1833 to fifty million in 1837. There were no increases, how-ever, from 1837 to 1849 and from that year until the end of Otho's reign agricultural production suffered severe reductions and Greece had to spend millions to import grains.[8]

The major problem which the Othonian court faced was finding a solution to utilize the National Estates which were an enormous potential source of revenue. The solution to that problem would have eliminated some of the Public Treasury's deficits and also the socio-economic weak-nesses of Greece. Brigandage and a massive landless section of the popu-lation were just two of the evils which an effective use of the National property could have eliminated. During the 1830s the Chamber of Depu-ties passed several laws which dealt with the distribution of the National Lands. In 1833 a Royal decree allowed each family to purchase land at the maximum value of two thousand drachmas, at six percent annual

interest payable in thirty-six years. The majority of the agrarian population could not afford to buy land. Those who could afford it, lost it after
several years of their purchase because of the existing tax structure.[9]
Many of those who bought land under the 1833 law sold their promisory
notes with a reduction of twenty to forty percent to usurers who were
usually the tax collectors or large landowners.[10]

In 1843 the government passed another law concerning the distribution
of the National Lands. The 1834 decree allowed the State to distribute
twenty to two hundred and forty stremmata of National property to
war veterans.[11] In 1838 a third law was enacted and it provided land
for the *Phalagites* (legionaires).[12] The government granted 105,836 stremmata to the war veterans and 163,608 to the *Phalagites*. Finally, Greece
distributed from 1821 to 1871 six hundred thousand stremmata to twenty
thousand refugee families who fled Turkish occupied territories. The
total number of National Lands distributed and sold from 1821 to 1871
was 870,444 strammata.

The question rarely asked by modern Greek historians is what use did
the Othonian government make of the National Estates? The answer is
reflected in the figures below:

Year	National Lands Revenue[13]
1834	572,772 drachmas
1838	844,274 drachmas
1840	1,016,360 drachmas
1843	805,636 drachmas

One year before Otho's exile the government utilized a little more than
one fourth of the total arable National Lands while the nation suffered
enormous trade deficits during King Otho's reign.[14]

Although it was true that during the Othonian era the Greek government did nothing to improve the nation's agricultural economy, the
blame for the nation's lack of agricultural progress must be shared equally
by the incompetent King Otho and his government as well as by the
British government and the bondholders of the 1824 and 1825 loans.
During Otho's reign the British government, pressured by the bondholders
of the first Greek loans, prevented Greece from alienating the National
lands. The Foreign Office argued that the National Estates were mortgaged

to the British bondholders and to the Powers for the loans of 1824, 1825 and 1832. The National property therefore could not be alienated until all the interest and sinking fund charges were completely paid to the Powers and the bondholders. The Foreign Office reminded Otho's government on numerous occasions in the 1840s and 1850s not to alienate the Crown property. During the Franco-British occupation, the Foreign Office prevented Greece from exercising her sovereignty over her own domains.

B.   *The British Bondholders and the National Estates*

In the fall of 1856 the Allied Powers attempted to impose financial controls in Greece. Franco-British troops still occupied the country although the Crimean War ended and a peace settlement agreed upon by the Powers.[15] In August 1956 Greece contemplated the sale of certain portions of the National property in order to increase the public revenue and reduce the budget deficit. Before the administration publically announced its plans in regards the sale of the National lands, intelligence sources informed the British Legation concerning the Greek government's plans. Once again Wyse and the Foreign Office were ready to exploit the vulnerability of the occupied Greek nation. The British Minister at Athens informed Lord Clarendon that the cabinet was in potential violation of the Treaty of 1832 for it contemplated the sale of the National property. He suggested to the Foreign Secretary that the three Powers must intervene and stop the government in Athens from carrying out its plans.[16]

There were many reasons behind Wyse's objection to the alienation of the National lands, but his concern with Greek violation of the 1832 treaty was certainly the least of all. First, the National Estates were mortgaged to the Powers for the guaranteed loan; second, they were mortgaged to the British bondholders of the 1824 and 1825 loans; and finally, the British government and the bondholders had not derived any benefit from the mortgaged National property ever since Greece became a kingdom. This was Wyse's reasoning which he wished the Greek government to know. It was not, however, the true reason for his objection to the alienation of the National Estates.

He knew that the Hellenic government distributed certain portions of its property since 1833 in order to raise revenue. The Public Treasury had not received the real value of the property which it sold to private citizens, and in most cases land was simply given away to Otho's friends. In any case, the alienation of government property yielded minimal revenues to the Public Treasury. The Greek government's argument that the sale of National property was necessary to raise revenues was a blatant lie as far as the British Legation was concerned. Land was simply used as an endowment for the King's friends who were Russophiles and anti-British. In September the Foreign Office instructed Wyse that the British government strongly opposed the alienation of the National Lands. Lord Clarendon charged that Greece contracted two loans in London in 1824 and 1825 but had not paid any interest to the bondholders ever since 1827.[17] Furthermore, the Foreign Secretary argued that Article XII of the 1832 treaty prohibited the sale of State property until the interest and sinking fund charges were paid to the Powers for the guaranteed loan. Technically, the British government used the Treaty of 1832 to prevent the Greek government from raising its public revenue by utilizing the National lands. This amounted to partial financial control. Lord Clarendon justified Great Britain's intervention in Greek financial affairs on the basis of the Greek government's failure to pay its foreign debt to the bondholders. He wrote:

> In August 1832 a public meeting was held in London by the Greek bondholders and Resolution passed relative to the Convention of May 1832, which were forwarded to the Greek government. It was stated in these Resolutions that the meeting observed that by the recent convention the first Revenues of Greece were pledged for the payment of the Interest of the loan then about to be raised, without any provision being made for the arrears due on the loans of 1824 and 1825, but the Revenues of Greece were pledged to the payment of the Interest and the National Lands to the redemption of the principal of the loans raised in 1824 and 1825, and that these resources should not be diverted from that object unless some satisfactory arrangement were made with the bondholders.[18]

British financiers and the Foreign Office exploited the financial weaknesses of Greece from 1824 to 1832 and during Otho's reign they imposed partial financial controls in Greece.

In September the cabinet at Athens submitted a *Projet du Loi* to the Chamber of Deputies for the distribution of National property. The proposed bill before the Chamber of Deputies allowed the government to alienate certain olive groves at Corinth and Salona as well as all the "perishable property." The administration and the Chambers wanted the passage of such a bill in order to stimulate agricultural production in the nation and expand the agrarian economic sector. The representatives of France and Great Britain at Athens formally protested to the Greek Foreign Ministry and objected to the bill before the Chamber. Mercier, the French minister at Athens, wrote to Alexander Ragabes, the Greek foreign minister, that the Crown property and all revenues which arose from it were mortgaged to the guaranteeing governments for the sixty million francs loan and therefore could not be alienated. The Hellenic government, Mercier maintained, should not have taken any action to sell portions of that property without prior consultation with the three Powers.[19] Wyse followed his French colleague's example and strongly protested against the sale of Crown property. He ascertained that the Protecting Powers had a right according to the Treaty of 1832 to claim the whole revenues of Greece arising from every source including the National lands. The Greek officials therefore had no right to sell the Crown property and totally disregarded their financial obligations to the Powers as well as to the bondholders. Like Mercier, Wyse informed Ragabes that the Greek government's prior consultation with the Powers was necessary if the administration in Athens wished to alienate any sector of the National property.[20]

Thomas Wyse believed that the Greek officials deceived the Powers because they labelled certain sectors of government property as "perishable lands." He explained to the Foreign Office that a large portion of the Greek territory which was covered with timber, the Administration erroneously but conveniently dismissed as "perishable." According to the British Legation, property did not have to be under cultivation or construction to be valuable as the Greeks maintained. The so-called "perishable lands" were enriched with timber and that alone made them useful.[21]

The Minister of Finance was disappointed when he was informed of the Western Powers' protestations. He stated to Ragabes that the National property was acquired by the Greek people who nourished it with their blood during the War of Independence. After a long struggle to regain their territory from the Ottoman empire the Western Protecting Powers prevented the Greeks from exercising sovereignty over their own land.[22] The minister of finance also stated that the Hellenic government only wanted to convert perishable, unproductive land, into revenue yielding property, in order to benefit the people and the State. He could not therefore understand why the Allied Powers objected to that action.[23]

The issue that worried the French and especially the British representatives at Athens was not only the reduction of the Crown property per se, but the politics involved in the alienation of these lands. In a confidential dispatch to Lord Clarendon, the British Charge d'Affaires outlined the major reasons why he thought that the sale of government property should have been unacceptable to Britain. (A) The Greek government disregarded the Allied Powers' protestations against the recent *Projet du Loi* concerning the sale of National property. (B) The Greek politicians act "under the patronage of the Court and of its partizans, and the proposed Laws are represented as emanating directly from her Majesty for the purpose of rewarding the heroes and sufferers of the revolution, developing national industry and augmenting the revenues of the State and that in these benevolent purposes, she (the Queen) is now thawrted by the selfish and anti-hellenic policy and ill-timed opposition of the two Western Governments."[24] As the above dispatch revealed, the Western Powers' inability to penetrate Greek politics and influence Court policy was at the heart of the National lands issue. The Western Powers never lost sight of their ultimate goal in Greece, namely, political, strategic and financial influence.

In an effort to counter British objections to the proposed bill before the Chamber of Deputies, Ragabes attempted to convince Wyse that Greece did not have the same obligation to Great Britain for the first two loans as she did for the loan of 1832. The Greek foreign minister claimed that his government's obligation to the bondholders was questionable. He did not deny the existence of the debt to the bondholders and their generosity, nor did he deny that the National Estates were indeed pledged as security to the bondholders for the repayment of the debt. He did, however, contend:

> (1) That the present government of Greece is not responsible
> for the engagements of the Revolutionary governments of 1824
> and 1825, and (2) that even admitting the debt still to hold good,
> the mortgage was null and void, as it was placed on Lands, the
> eventual possession of which was doubtful, and a considerable
> portion of which was actually not included in the kingdom of
> Greece, but forms, on the contrary, at this moment a part of
> Turkey.[25]

In response to this argument, Wyse maintained that the history of Greece
could not be ignored. He stated that the Kapodistrian government acknowledged responsibility for the 1824 and 1825 debt. The assembly at
Argos in 1829 also claimed responsibility for the Greek debt to the bondholders, and declared that the National Estates were mortgaged for the
first Greek loans. Furthermore, Wyse claimed, that the Regency of 1834
fully acknowledged the Greek responsibility to the bondholders. The
Voulgaris administration, Wyse concluded, had the same responsibility
for its foreign debts as did all the previous Greek governments.

Since Ragabes failed to convince the British Minister by appealing to
history he used a different approach still determined to gain British
permission for the sale of the state property. He argued that the alienation of National property was inevitable because the administration of
16/28 May 1854, promised a number of Greek families the endowment
of land. The King delivered a speech before the Chamber of Deputies
concerning this issue in May 1854 which the Voulgaris administration
could not possibly reverse and was thus forced the act upon it.[26] Furthermore, Ragabes remined Wyse, that the Chamber of Deputies passed a
law in 1834 for the alienation of perishable lands, and it was urgent that
unproductive property be converted to yield income for the Greek people
and the State.[27]

Wyse remained unconvinced by Ragabes' arguments. He believed that
the cabinet created all sorts of justifications for the alienation of State
property to please the Court. In response to the Greek foreign minister's
claim that previous administrations passed laws concerning the alienation
of National property therefore the sale had to be carried out in the present,

Wyse maintained that the cabinet at Athens deliberately hurried the passage of the bill in September so that the Powers would not have the opportunity to examine it. Furthermore, Wyse argued that the Greek state could not have taken such action without first consulting the guaranteeing governments.[28] Ragabes stated that the Powers never asked to examine the bill, and when they finally did ask, it was already on the floor before the Chambers for consideration and the cabinet could not have taken action to retard the legislative process in the Chambers.[29] The British Minister who had informants within the Greek government,[30] knew that this was not true. In reality the Chamber of Deputies took their orders from the cabinet and the cabinet followed Otho's policy. Wyse therefore, refused to accept further arguments on the subject and made it clear to Ragabes that his government's final decision was against allowing Greece to alienate any part of the National property.[31]

When the Protecting Powers established the Financial Commission in 1857,[32] one of the first demands which their representatives placed before the Greek Ministry of Finance was for a complete survey of the National Estates. Precise statistics were not submitted to the Financial Commission but the Ministry of Finance submitted a report which outlined the extent and distribution of the government's domain. The survey below reflected the distribution of the National lands. (1) To refugees who took part in the War of Independence and whose countries do not include today part of the Greek domains; (2) to inactive officers, noncommissioned officers, soldiers and all military personnel of land and sea; (3) to policemen; (4) for political endowments; (5) for a ten-year credit; (6) for the academics; (7) for settlement and colonies; (8) in favor of National lots used to erect government buildings or for repair of public buildings; (9) to legionaire and naval endowments; (10) in favor of firebrand; (11) for orphanage endowments; (12) in favor of individuals who excelled during the struggle for independence; (13) for construction of cities; (14) towards application of city planning; (15) in favor of Farmers.[33]

According to the officials in Athens the distribution of the Crown property to public and private sectors was necessary and justifiable for a resurgent nation which lacked vital public buildings and whose population was landless.

The dispossessed, the war heroes, and the agricultural community of the resurgent nation cried out for the redistribution of land. The government therefore was pressured from the public to distribute the National lands while simultaneously it was pressured from the Powers and the bond-holders not to aliente it. The government tried to compromise between the domestic and foreign forces as much as it could. The Powers, however, only opposed the alienation of the State property when the administration attempted to mortgage it for a loan which the bondholders and the guar-anteeing governments disapproved, or when the King wished to sell or grant property to his friends. They did not object to the Greek govern-ment's efficient use of the lands which could have enriched the Public Treasury. So it would be unfair to place all the blame on the Powers for the undeveloped National Estates when the administrations during the Othonian era did nothing to improve the status of that property.

During the establishment of the Financial Commission (1875-1859) the British bondholders used the opportunity to force Greece to pay her debt on the 1824 and 1825 loans. The bondholders were concerned with Greece's neglect to pay any interest on their loans and they requested the Foreign Office on several occasions in 1858 to intervene on their behalf and settle the issue through the Commission. Wyse, who was one of the three members of the Commission, was asked by the bondholders to represent their interests in Greece. The British Charge d'Affaires pro-mised them that his Legation would force Greece to accept the legality of the bondholders' claims and that after the Commission's investigations were concluded he would be in a favorable position to demand from the Greek State a just settlement for the bondholders' claims.

In its concluding report the Commission did not make any recommen-dations to Greece on the bondholders' debt settlement. The reason for this was that the Commission was a body which represented the interests of the three Powers and not those of individual financiers who had un-settled debts with Greece. Nevertheless the following remarks on the Commission's final report indirectly attacked the Greek government's irresponsible policy toward the bondholders.

> That every year the mass of arrears, which involves an indefinite number of debtors in liability to the revenue, assumes more vast proportions; that the laws destined for these arrears have been inefficacious;[35]

The bondholders appointed C. N. Merlin to represent them in Greece and especially to seek fulfillment of their claims. He was, however, unable to accomplish a great deal due to the Commission's investigations and goals which prevented representation of special interest groups.[36] The bondholders' debt remained unresolved therefore during Otho's reign.

The final confrontation between Greece and the British bondholders during Otho's reign occurred in 1862, the year of Otho's exile. In February the Government attempted to raise a two million drachmas loan from the National Bank of Greece. As security the state pledged portions of the National Estates, certain olive groves, and part of the Custom House duties.[37] When the British Legation's intelligence sources confirmed the rumors that a loan was indeed under negotiation between the Greek State and the National Bank, C. N. Merlin wrote to Wyse "to protest against any further alienation of the National Lands of Greece."[38] The Greek government secretly negotiated a loan without prior consultation with the Powers' representatives. Officials in Greece knew that Britain and perhaps France and Russia would raise serious protests against the proposed loan.

Wyse who was the first to find out about it and to object to it, contacted G. Koundouriotes, the foreign minister, in February and protested against the alienation of National Estates on behalf of Merlin and the bondholders. He also requested to know the Greek official position on the unconfirmed rumors concerning the loan and finally stated that if the administration planned to raise a loan it was in violation of "the security guaranteed to the three Powers for the loan made to Greece under the Convention of 1832."[39] The Greek Foreign Minister confirmed the rumors concerning the loan and stated that Greece intended to use perishable lands as security for the two million drachmas. Like previous administrations the 1862 cabinet argued that the government was at liberty to alienate any portions of the National Estates which were considered perishable.[40] The Russian and the French governments joined the British and protested against the proposed loan and the alienation of the state property. The Powers' concerted efforts against Greece in 1862 occurred for the first time during Otho's reign, but in 1862 Otho was so unpopular with the European community that even Prince Gorchakoff, the Russian foreign minister who supported the Greek monarch, recognized the bondholders' legitimate claims in Greece.[41]

During Otho's reign the bondholders had not received any interest payments from Greece. The government in Athens totally ignored its debt to the British financiers who in 1824 and 1825 extended their aid to the struggling nation. The result of the government's failure to respond to the bondholders' claims was one of the reasons that Great Britain did not allow Greece to extend her sovereignty over her own domain. The loans of 1824 and 1825 had ill-effects in Greece throughout Otho's reign and beyond it. Interest for the first loans had accumulated to 4,147, 375 pounds sterling in 1863, one year after Otho's exile.[42] By 1878 the country owed to the bondholders 10,030,000 pounds sterling.[43] Otho's contribution to the Greek foreign debt was enormous but he alone cannot take all the blame. Those who contracted the loans and misappropriated the funds were also equally guilty for burdening the nation with a huge foreign debt. Great Britain who used the bondholders' claim for political reasons and hindered economic progress in Greece by imposing controls on the National Estates must also take her share of the blame. In the final analysis the British as well as the other two Protecting Powers were responsible for violating the Treaty of 1832 which guaranteed Greece's sovereignty as a free nation.

CHAPTER IV

THE FINANCIAL COMMISSION AND OTHO'S EXILE

A. *The Proposal*

The Crimean War ended early in 1856 and Greece was no longer a threat to the Allied Powers. At the Paris Peace Conference in February 1856, however, the Greek government was not represented and the Franco-British occupation continued after the peace settlement. The Western Powers occupied Greece illegally even though it was no longer a threat to them. This was due to their resentment of the persistent pro-Russian attitude of Otho and the cabinet in Athens.[1] The Greek monarch succeeded in the fall of 1855 to eliminate the "Ministry of occupation," headed by Mavrokordatos, and replaced it with the Demitris Voulgaris administration.[2] The new administration was composed of Francophiles and Russophiles all loyal supporters of King Otho and his policies.[3] The Greek monarch still entertained an expansionist foreign policy and the Franco-British occupation had not altered his pro-Russian and anti-British sentiments.[4] In order to dissuade the King from supporting any further anti-Turkish activities and alter his attitude about Russia the Allied Powers prolonged the occupation one year after the Paris Peace Conference.

The prolonged occupation made the Greek government and the nation in general more anti-British than ever before so the Greek Court had the peoples' support in its policies. After the Mavrokordatos Ministry fell the Foreign Office resumed financial pressures on Greece hoping that Otho and his government would give in to British political influence. In March 1856 Wyse complained to the Foreign Office that the cabinet at

Athens was irresponsible in her financial relations with the Great Powers.
He wrote to Lord Clarendon:

> The government has, I regret to say, reverted to the old financial
> falacy, and allowed the advances of the Three Powers to enter
> into the statement as if it were revenue an absurdity discarded
> by the Mavrodordatos Ministry and serving no purpose but to
> flatter or mislead. There has been no intimation given to me or
> to my French colleague of any payments to be mde, interest or
> principal on account of the Laon, pursuant to the Treaty of
> 1832. On the contrary, it is assumed that the indulgence granted
> under such special circumstances to the late government, has
> virtually been continued to this without a word pronounced by
> them or deserved by us on the subject.[5]

Wyse also reported that the Greek finances were in a most lamentable
condition and that Greece was very far from achieving any economic
or financial stability.

The British minister criticized the Voulgaris administration's financial
policy for political reasons, but there was sufficient evidence which indicated that the 1856 Ministry expected the same favoritism from the
Allied Powers as the Mavrokordatos Ministry enjoyed. As a result of this
deception, the Voulgaris administration neglected the country's foreign
debt. According to a Greek government report of 1856 the Powers should
have received 805,886.70 francs for the first six-month instalment on the
interest and sinking fund of the loan. The first chart on the following
pages (72 and 73) composed by the Greek Ministry of Finance in 1856
outlined the sum which each Power advanced for the guaranteed loan
from 1838 to 1855 on behalf of Greece, and the second outlined the
interest, sinking fund and commission, advanced by the three Powers
from 1833 until 1 March 1856.

In twenty-three years the Greek foreign debt to the guaranteeing Powers climbed to a level that Greece could not possibly afford to repay.
The Western Powers were reluctant therefore to lift the occupation especially when the King and Cabinet continued to antagonize them and
refuse their political patronage.

In March the Greek Minister in Paris asked Count Walewski, the French
foreign minister, who succeeded Drouyn de Lhuys, when France intended

to remove her troops from Athens. Walewski responded that Greece still entertained Russian sympathies and the administration in Athens had not abandoned its anti-Turkish foreign policy. Furthermore, he urged that the Greek government should not neglect its financial obligations to the Powers and should pay the interest charges on the loan annually after it had satisfied its most urgent expenses.[7] France, therefore, was unwilling to remove the occupation in Greece because of the government's aggressive foreign policy and neglect of the foreign debt.

Great Britain was even more reluctant than France to lift the occupation from Athens and Wyse was more pessimistic about Greek finances than his colleagues at the Greek capital. In April he suggested to the British Foreign Secretary that the Powers should intervene in Greek internal affairs in order to improve the country's financial situation. The British Charge d'Affaires criticized severely King Otho and blamed him for the existing corruption and intrigue in the government and also for the nation's financial and economic regression. Wyse charged that the King abused his power, violated the Constitution of 1843 and carried out policies counterproductive to Greek national interests. Furthermore, he reiterated the Powers' obligation and duty under the Treaty of 1832 to intervene in Greek internal affairs for the improvement and the general welfare of Greece. He wrote to Clarendon:

> On the honor and duty of the Protecting Powers on their side
> it is needless to speak; the Greeks comprehend both; they think
> that we have a right to require under the Treaty of 1832, good
> government, and that we are bound to require it by a sense of
> our own dignity, and by our obligations to this country and to
> Europe. How it is to be obtained, is another question . . . .[8]

As early as spring 1856 Wyse suggested to the Foreign Office that the Powers should directly intervene in the Greek government in order to bring it under their control. He had not thought of financial control early in 1856 for he was too concerned with achieving British political control as was the case from May 1854 to September 1855 with the Mavrokordatos Ministry. He gradually realized, however, that political control was impossible because the French and the Russians would protest against British interference in Greek internal affairs and thus the Powers' conflict would leave Otho more powerful to exercise his own policies.

TABLE A

Dette de la Grèce envers les trois Puissances garantes de l'emprunt

	Trésor Anglais	Trésor Russe
Avançes faites par le Trésor français en 1838, 1839 et 1840, pour le service des obligations par lui garanties		
Advances faites par les trois Puissances pour le service de l'emprunt depuis l'année 1843 jusqu'au 1er September 1855.	14,347,382.36	15,422,329.97
Idem pour le semestre échu le 1er Mars.	595,164.15	605,987.05
TOTAL.	14,942,546.51	16,028,317.02

	Trésor Français	Ensemble
Avançes faites par le Trésor français en 1838, 1839 et 1840, pour le service des obligations par lui garanties.	2,762,444.70	2,762,444.70
Avançes faites par les trois Puissances por le service de l'emprunt depuis l'annee 1843 jusqu'au 1er September 1855.	13,270,491.10	43,040,203.43
Idem pour le semestre échu le 1er Mars.	522,019.83	1,723,171.03
TOTAL.	16,554,955.63	47,525,819.16

TABLE B

Le service de l'emprunt s'est opéré par paiemens semistriels, començant six mois aprés le 1er September 1833, c'est à dire le 1er Mars 1834. Depuis cette époque jusqu'au 1er Mars 1856, les semestres successivement échus (y compris celui du 1er Mars 1856) ont absorbé une sommes de Fr. 72, 590,432.08 composée come suite:

	garantie Anglaise	garantie Russe
Interets a 5 pour %	20,742,463.92	20,842,508.66
Amortissement a 1 pour %	4,148,492.53	4,168,501.55
	24,890,956.45	25,011,010.21
Commission 1 pour %.	248,909.48	250,109.72
Ensemble.	25,139,865.93	25,261,119.93
Frais d'insertion dans les journaux et autres menus frais	14,320.17	14,320.17
TOTAL.	25,154,186.10	25,275,440.10

	garantie Française	Ensemble pour les 3 garanties
Interets a 5 pour %	18,272,678.25	59,857,650.83
Amortissement a 1 pou %	3,654,535.55	11,971,529.63
	21,927,213.80	71,829,180.46
Commission 1 pour %.	219,271.91	718,291.11
Ensemble.	22,146,485.71	72,547,471.57
Frais d'insertion dans les journaux et autres menus frais	14,320.17	42,960.51
TOTAL.	22,160,805.88	72,590,432.08

Pendent le même période les operations des fonds d'amortissement, agissant tantôt par voie de remboursement au apir a le suite de tirages au sort, tantôt par voie de rachats aux Bourses de Paris, et Londres, lorsque le cours des obligations était au dessous de pair, ont produit les resultats.[6]

The British representative at Athens, dissatisfied with the Persistent Pro-Russian attitudes in Greece, increased his concern with direct British intervention in Greek internal affairs. In June he criticized the King and his Court and repeated to the Foreign Office Otho's negative attitude toward the Western Powers. He emphasized the need for France and Great Britain to change the present political and financial condition of Greece. Since the Powers had the right by Treaty to be concerned with the future of their Protectorate, Wyse reasoned, then the only question which demanded an answer was "how to employ our *right* and power of intervention."[9] Of course Wyse claimed in most of his dispatches to the Foreign Office that the reasons for more direct intervention by the Powers in Greece were to improve the government, the economy and bring internal peace, prosperity and freedom to the Greek nation. The British Legation in Athens, however, was not concerned with the Greek national interests but only with carrying out British policy. Wyse was correct for blaming Otho and the Greek Court for the majority of the problems which faced Greece. It is beyond doubt, however, that the reason for his opposition to the Greek Court was due to the pro-Russian and anti-British policies which the King entertained and not to Wyse's concern for Greek progress.[10]

In June 1856 Wyse proposed the "removal of the Camarilla" (as he labelled the Greek Court) from Greece. The Powers had to take extreme measures according to the British Legation because the Greek monarchical power with the Germanic countries at its side[11] humble the Powers influence in Greece.[12] Finally, there was the issue of the unpaid instalments which Greece owed to the Powers and Wyse believed that the Greek Court took advantage of the Powers' generosity. He wrote to the Foreign Secretary:

> . . . are we who are so punctilious about the addition of 10 or 20 pounds sterling a year to a clerk, to pay annually to King Otho £47,000 to enable him with impunity to govern this country, to its and our detriment, returning us for our forbearance, but resistance to our admonitions and contempt for our threats? It is not Greece which is our tributary, but we are tributaries to Greece; What then, in conclusion is to be our future policy? One of two courses. Direct and effectual intervention so as to compel,

if we cannot persuade King and government to do right;
power in fine, real and effectual if we are to undertake the
responsibility of directing the country.[13]

It was not at all surprising that Wyse made such a blunt recommendation
to the Foreign Office in view of Greek-British relations since the Armansperg dismissal.

Wyse failed to realize, however, that Great Britain in collaboration with
Russia and France selected Prince Otho and forced him upon Greece.
Furthermore, he was so eager to please the Foreign Office and its policy
which Greece obstructed in the Near East, that he was willing to violate
the Treaty of 1832 by having the Powers directly intervene into Greek
internal affairs. So while he claimed that Greece violated the terms of the
Treaty of 1832 because she did not discharge her instalment payments to
the Powers, the French and British also violated the same Treaty from
May 1854 to February 1857 when they occupied Greece. Wyse was not
satisfied with the occupation, however, and asked his government to
further violate Greek sovereignty and intervene "more directly and
effectively." in Greek affairs.

The Foreign Office was receptive to its Legation's recommendations
for the reasons which Wyse outlined. There were, however, more than
political, and financial reasons which caused Clarendon to embrace the
notiorious Wyse proposal. In 1845 Greek imports reached 22,300,000
drachmas, and nine million of the nation's total imports came from Great
Britain. In 1849 the total imports were 20,799,501 drachmas but Greece
imported goods amounting six million from England while it increased
her import and export trade with the Ottoman empire and Egypt.[14]
British citizens had economic interests in Greece who exploited the emery
mines of Naxos,[15] imported the currants of Corinth[16] had investments
in the National Lands, and engaged in other business transactions with
Greece. The British government blockaded Greece in 1850 partially to
protect the economic interests of its citizens and during Otho's reign it
claimed that it wished to continue providing that protection.

Wyse and the Foreign Office were aware that France and especially
Russia would never have condoned the Protecting Powers' direct intervention in Greece. In July the British Charge d' Affaires at Athens devised
a plan which he believed would have been appealing to the other two

Powers. According to the new plan the basis for the Powers' intervention was Article XII paragraph six of the Treaty. Since Greece had not lived up to the terms of the Treaty in regards to Article XII the Powers' representatives at Athens had the right to watch over Greek finances. Thomas Wyse recommended that the Powers had the right to demand that "none of the actual receipts of the Greek Treasury shall be employed for any other purpose until those payments shall be secured for the current year."[17] Greece, he concluded, should be forced by the guaranteeing governments to abide by this stipulation.

A literal execution of Wyse's proposal would have drained Greek finances and destroyed the government. The British representative insisted, however, that the Powers would never be repaid for the guaranteed loan if they waited to receive the surplus of the Greek revenues. Wyse stated that he and his French and Russian colleagues at Athens should be authorized to form a "Commission of inquiry into Greek finances, that is into their (Greek) former and actual amount and application, how far income can be increased and expenditure diminished and in what way the means to attain this double object can be brought into prompt and effective operation."[18] The Commission as Wyse conceived of it intended to prevent Greece from further violations of Article XII of the 1832 Treaty. At the same time, however, the Commission which was conceived as an instrument of European financial control in Greece violated the same Treaty which guaranteed Greece her sovereignty.

The Greek government which was warned about its international financial policy by the Allied Powers took radical measures to liquidate the foreign debt and prevent any foreign intervention in its finances. Alexander Ragabes felt that the loan of 1832 did enormous damage to the nation while it brought few benefits. He reminded Spyridon Trikoupis, the Greek ambassador in London, that Britain should note the benefit of the guaranteed loan was less than ten percent of the principal or six million drachmas. The Greek Foreign Minister complained that such a small amount contributed little to Greek economic progress and the Powers knew it; Yet they coersed Greece knowing of her financial weaknesses.[19] Ragabes proposed a plan to prevent any further coersive measures by the Powers. Beginning in 1857, he stated, that the Greek government would grant one hundred thousand drachmas annually to each Power; beginning in 1862 the amount would be increased to two hundred thousand and five years after 1862 Greece would issue six hundred thousand drachmas to each Power until the entire debt was paid.[20]

Trikoupis met with the British Foreign Secretary and informed him of Ragabes' message concerning the Greek government's attitude toward the loan and the proposed plan for the liquidation of the country's foreign debt. Trikoupis also stated that his nation was in great financial distress and in desperate need of material progress.[21] Clarendon assured the Greek ambassador that he sympathized with Greece and fully understood the country's difficulties. He expressed his personal admiration for Greek progress in commerce, navigation and agriculture. Clarendon's statements were private and unofficial so Trikoupis advised his government that they did not reflect Great Britain's foreign policy in Greece.[22]

The Greek ambassador in London, however, was more confused by his own government's statements than he was by Clarendon's favorable unofficial comments about Greece. On 14/26 July, Ragabes sent to the Greek embassy in London a payment plan for the debt on the guaranteed loan, and asked Trikoupis to submit it to the Foreign Office. Five days later the administration changed that plan because it believed that it could not afford the annual payments indicated, and thus reduced them. An outline of plans A and B were as follows:

Plan A [23]

Year	Sums to each Power
From 1857	300,000 drachmas
From 1861	600,000 drachmas
From 1865	900,000 drachmas
From 1869	1,000,000 drachmas

Plan B

Year	Sums to each Power
From 1857	100,000 drachmas
From 1862	200,000 drachmas
From 1867	600,000 drachmas

The Finance Ministry reported to Ragabes that the total debt for the guaranteed loan in 1856 amounted to 72,590,432 francs.[24] When he made up the original plan he had that figure in mind but he considered that Greece only received 6,193,722.60 drachmas from the principal of the loan. He also considered Otho's reluctance to give in to Franco-British financial pressure, therefore he reduced the payments on his second instalment plan.[25]

Clarendon and Walewski did not accept either plan. They both wanted a serious inquiry into Greek finances in order to obtain a permanent settlement on the Greek foreign debt.[26] In September Phocion Roques, the Greek representative at Paris, informed Ragabes that the French government agreed with the proposal of a Financial Commission as the solution to Greek financial chaos and as a means for the Power to settle their financial differences with Greece. The Cabinet in Athens was appaled with the suggestion of the occupying Powers. Ragabes believed that France and Great Britain violated Greek sovereignty in May 1854 when they occupied Greece, then the Allied Powers illegally prolonged the occupation after the Paris Peace Conference and finally they wanted to damage the occupied nation's freedom by imposing financial controls. The Foreign Minister warned the Allied Powers through the Greek embassies in London and Paris that the Financial Commission's establishment would have a negative impact on the Greek people who were already dissilusioned about the role of France and Great Britain in Greece.[27] Furthermore, he charged that the Commission would be used by the Powers' Legations in Athens as an instrument to interfere in the domestic politics of Greece.

Trikoupis tried his utmost to convince Clarendon of the Greek financial difficulties. He maintained that Greece suffered economically because of the three year Allied occupation, of the rising brigandage throughout the country, and of the substantial reduction in agriculture, and in commerce and navigation as a result of the Crimean War. The government in Athens, Trikoupis added, needed time to make the payments on the interest on the loan because from the year that Greece became a kingdom her Treasury suffered enormous deficits.[28] Finally, the Greek representative at London submitted his government's third payment plan for the debt's liquidation. From 1857 until 1861 Greece proposed to pay the three Powers a total of 300,000 drachmas, from 1862 until 1866 600,000, from 1867 until 1871; 900,000 and from 1872 until the entire amount was paid, 1,000,000 drachmas.[29] The purpose of this final offer was to avoid the Financial Commission's establishment but the Western Powers had plans of their own and refused to accept Ragabes' offer. In a confidential dispatch to the Greek Foreign Ministry Trikoupis informed the Cabinet at Athens that the French and the British agreed on the establishment of a Financial Commission whose purpose was the examination of Greek finances. The Western Powers also submitted that proposal to Russia for her response.[30]

Meanwhile Wyse in Athens continued to produce evidence against the weaknesses of Greek finances and the Administration's neglect of the foreign debt. He pressed the Foreign Office to carry out the plan of a Commission. He urged that if the guaranteeing governments had any hope of receiving payments from Greece they had to force Greece to pay her debts. He maintained, however, that once established the Commission would not be taken seriously by Greek politicians unless the Powers fully supported it. He wrote to Clarendon confidentially:

> To make it (the Commission) effective the Court and government should really *fear it,* and not consider it a diplomatic expenditure to get rid of a difficulty .... If on the contrary, it is determined to go searchingly and extensively into every branch of government ... it may effect these important objects; it will be a reality; it will bring out to view, a large map of abuse and incapacity, and allow time to mature other plans, and to base them on what I have little doubt, will be a most justifying authority.[31]

In the same dispatch Wyse explained the political reasons for the Commission's establishment.

The Voulgaris Ministry was composed mainly of Russophiles and a few Francophiles. The King favored Russian diplomacy in the Near East and opposed the British. Wyse feared a pro-Russian domination in all sectors of Greek government. According to him the politicians in the Chamber of Deputies, the local politicians, government bureaucrats and Court advisors were all pro-Russian. He concluded that the Russian influence had penetrated Greece through the nation's politics, the press, religion and the Court. This was an important diplomatic consideration for Britain who always feared Russian expansionist policy in the Near East. Wyse recommended to the Foreign Office that the prolonged occupation was therefore necessary to prevent Otho from becoming a puppet of the Russians. "We have no choice," he wrote, "but to remain as we are; the weak must bow to the stronger."[32] The Commission's establishment from the British and to a lesser extent French viewpoints was necessary and inevitable upon removal of the occupying forces in Athens, in order to secure a balance of power in Greece between the three guaranteeing governments.

Ragabes protested to the Foreign Office that the Commission would create popular indignation in Greece and that it would compromise the kingdom's natural independence and prosperity. He also criticized the prolonged Anglo-Gallic occupation of Greece and added that the Commission which would be authorized to investigate every government department would be worse than the occupation.[33] Wyse responded to the Greek Foreign Minister's charges as follows:

> The Greek government ought to thank the Protecting Powers
> for having adopted a course so much short of their legitimate
> rights, as a preliminary inquiry . . . .[34]

In November the Cabinet at Athens submitted the 1857 budget to the Chamber of Deputies with an increase in expenditure of 1,319,673.22 drachmas over the 1856 budget. Wyse used the increase in the 1857 budget to prove the Cabinet's wasteful financial practices and to convince the Foreign Office that a Financial Commission was necessary.[35]

In order to clarify the purpose, and function of the Financial Commission Clarendon instructed Lord Cowley, British ambassador at Paris, to explain to Walewski Britain's concept of the Commission. The British Foreign Secretary wanted Russian and French approval of the Commission before its establishment. Clarendon argued that the Greek government provided him with a proposal to discharge its foreign debt owed to the Powers. He claimed, however, that the Protecting governments had a legitimate right to assure themselves that Greece would strictly obey its own proposal. A joint Commission of the three Powers in Athens therefore would be authorized to take cognizance of the Greek government's financial measures in which the Public funds were administered.[36] The

Foreign Secretary further added that if Greek finances improved under the Commission's supervision, and there was revenue surplus, then the Powers' representatives would decide whether that surplus should go toward repayment of the Greek foreign debt or as the three Powers' plenipotentiaries decided.

Count Walewski reacted strongly against the British proposal of the Financial Commission. He believed that the Foreign Office's proposal violated Greek sovereignty because it gave unrestrained power to the Commission. The French Foreign Minister argued that Britain favored European financial control in Greece but this was neither necessary nor possible. Furthermore, Count Walewski disagreed with Clarendon on several other points concerning the Commission's establishment. First, he did not believe, as did the British Foreign Secretary, that the Commission would have created economic and financial regeneration in Greece, dissolved government corruption and converted the nation from poverty to prosperity. Secondly, he stated that Greece and Russia would never agree to the British proposal and they would have accused Britain of violating the Treaty of 1832. Finally, he doubted if the Protecting Powers had the right in accordance with international practice to exercise such inquisitorial power over an independent state as the Foreign Office proposed. Given these factors the proposed Commission, according to Walewski, was doomed to failure and the Western Powers would have found it increasingly more difficult to resume normal relations with their Protectorate.[37]

The French Foreign Minister proposed his own plan which he believed the Russians and the Greeks would accept. His proposal called for the "withdrawal of the troops of occupation, the resumption of a common understanding at Athens between the three Protecting Powers, and such an examination of the finances of Greece as the position of the three Powers, as creditors of the State, warranted."[38] Cowley insisted that Walewski's plan was too moderate and a more rigid proposal was necessary to grant the Commission more authority. He argued that Russia exercised enormous influence in Greece in all sectors of the county and it was not in the best interests of the Western Powers to allow Russian expansionism in the Balkans, especially after the Crimean War. Walewski did not share Clarendon's and Britain's Russophobia and was not convinced that Russia had as much influence in Greece as the British liked to believe. He retained therefore his position on the proposal of a moderately empowered Commission.[39]

Clarendon realized that the French proposal would be more readily acceptable to Russia and Greece than the British proposal. He renounced his original plan therefore and accepted Walewski's terms for the Commission's establishment. Russia opposed any measures of Western European financial control in Greece and Prince Gorchokoff expressed his disatisfaction with Franco-British occupation in Greece on several occasions since the Paris Peace Conference.[40] The Tsar's government, however, was not in the position after the Crimean War of exercising much influence in the decision making process concerning the Powers' policy in Greece. The St. Petersburg government instructed Count Creptowitch, the Russian ambassador in London, to express Russia's gratitude to Clarendon for renouncing his original plan concerning the Financial Commission and accepting the French proposal.[41] The Russian government agreed that the Powers' Resident Ministers at Athens, assisted by financial experts, would form a Commission of financial inquiry in Greece.[42]

In order to secure the liquidation of the Greek foreign debt the guaranteeing governments agreed that their respective Resident Ministers at Athens were authorized to request and receive all the necessary information from the Greek government. Lord Clarendon instructed Wyse that the Commissioners' purpose would be to:

> . . . judge with regard to the due employment of the public funds and to offer suggestions for the improvement of the general financial administration of the country. Nevertheless it is not the intention of the British and French governments that the Commission should interfere directly with the administration of the Greek finances; its action would be to watch over the execution of the financial measures adopted by the Greek government and to report to the respective governments the results of its observations. The course which the governments of England and France are thus prepared to adopt cannot lead to any undue interference in the financial affairs of Greece.[43]

This resolution was only accepted by the Foreign Office after France, Russia and the Germanic Powers applied intensive diplomatic pressure on Britain to prevent her from establishing a Commission in Greece with unlimited authority.[44]

One of the most serious problems for Greece in 1856 was the prolonged Franco-British occupation. The Western Powers refused to remove their fleets from Pireaus until after the Commission's establishment. Russia, however, protested that the presence of Anglo-French troops in Greece during the time of peace constituted a serious violation of Hellenic independence. Furthermore, the Tsar's government objected to the Western Powers' insistence that the Commission should be a permanent body in Greece and not temporary. The Russian Foreign Minister instructed Count Risseloff, Russian ambassador at Paris, to protest against the "permanent" establishment of the Commission and that word should be eliminated from the agreement. Risseloff stated to Walewski that Greek independence was threatened if the Powers insisted on a "permanent" Commission. He argued that such an organization could only lead to the Powers' financial control in Greece. Finally, the Russian Ambassador asked that the Powers should be compassionate toward their Protectorate which had limited economic resources and weak state finances.[45]

Walewski agreed with Russia that the word "permanent" should be detatched from the agreement concerning the Commission. He informed the French Legation at Athens that it should note the change in regards to the Commission's temporary status[46] and after Risseloff persuaded him, Walewski asked the Foreign Office to concur with the Russian modification. He also asked the British goverment to consider plans for the Allied troops' removal from Athens.[47] The British agreed to omit the word "permanent" from the Financial Commission[48] knowing Russian resentment of British policy in Greece and French willingness to curb Britain's ambitions in the Levant. Lord Palmerston, who was Prime Minister, secretly supported the Wyse plan concerning financial control in Greece through the establishment of the Financial Commission,[49] but there was little he could do since France sided with Russia on this issue. The British government finally agreed with the other two Protecting Powers that once the Greek economy was revitalized and the country's finances were in order the Commission would cease its functions.[50]

In January 1857 the Greek government reluctantly accepted the Financial Commission and it agreed to "furnish without reserve and with the greatest promptitude all information which may relate to the task which the Commission has to fulfill."[51] According to the Powers' agreement, Greece was required to submit all the documents which the Commission requested. If the Greek government refused to cooperate, the Commission would then appeal to the Protecting Powers to enforce their decision. Each Minister of the respective guaranteeing governments had equal authority in the Commission so no one Legation could exert excessive pressure on the host government.[52] Greece was placed in a situation which made it necessary for its government to accept the Commission or face permanent occupation by the Western Powers. The King's and the Cabinet's willingness to be rid of the Anglo-Gallic forces in Athens drove them to the decision of accepting the Financial Commission.

In December 1856, Great Britain and France started plans for the occupation's removal knowing it would be replaced with the Commission. To speed up the process Greece assured the British and French governments that portions of the country's resources would be dedicated for the annual instalment payments on the interest and sinking fund due to the Powers.[53] At the end of January Greece agreed to the Commission's establishment but Palmerston and Walewski did not order their troops out of Pireaus. The French Foreign Minister pressured by Russia and Greece ordered the French fleet in Pireaus to prepare for evacuation of Greek soil. The French government informed Britain of its evacuation plans in Greece and urged Clarendon to issue the same order to the British fleet at Pireaus.[54] Before the British troops evacuated Pireaus, Lord Clarendon justified the prolonged illegal occupation of Greece to the British Parliament as necessary due to the numerous brigandage incidents in the country. He also justified the need for a Financial Commission. The Foreign Secretary argued that the Greek government's inability to manage its own finances forced the Powers to install a Commission so that the Administration in Athens would resume its annual instalment payments to the guaranteeing governments for the 1832 loan. Finally, Lord Clarendon reassured Parliament that the Powers did not intend to interfere in Greek domestic affairs through the Commission.[55]

B.   The Inquiries

On 18 February 1857, the Financial Commission held its first meeting at the British Legation in Athens. Wyse was elected President and M. de Greling, the Secretary of the French Legation, as Secretary to the Commission. Wyse informed the Hellenic government of the Commission's initiation and asked Ragabes to appoint a high ranking official to act as an intermediary between the Commission and the government in Athens and provide the information which he and his colleagues would request.[56] Originally the three Powers had agreed to have one Greek representative on the Commission to secure equal representation in the process of inquiries by the Powers representatives.[57] That plan, however, was abandoned and the three resident Ministers at Athens had more freedom to probe into Greek finances.

The Commission outlined its purpose to the Greek government as follows:

1' Examen des diverses branches du revenue et des resources du pays.
2. Examen du mode de perfection de ce revenue.
3. Examen depenses de l'État.
4. Examen des reformes que l'on peut proposer.[58]

The Commission's President sent a copy of the above dispatch to Ragabes and asked him to submit a statement of the budgets of 1844 and 1857 along with a statement of all perishable property.[59]

Although the three Powers agreed before the Commission's establishment that it would not be permanent and it would not be used as an instrument of financial control, Wyse had different plans. He was suspicious of the host government's misunderstanding of the Commission as simply a ceremonial financial investigative body which was powerless to interfere in Greek internal affairs. He was more than anxious to correct that misconception. He wrote to Clarendon:

> The Commission was not limited to an inquiry into the expendiecny of accepting or not Mr. Ragabes' proposition, but that on the contrary, it held itself wholly disengaged from that or any other proposal of the Greek government from any portion of

the interest due or to be due on the loan, or to apply any portion thereof to the encouregement of Greek involvements, but consider itself perfectly free to adopt any course which a serious and comprehensive inquiry into the whole financial condition might point out.[60]

According to the Powers' understanding and agreement concerning the Commission, Wyse and his colleagues in Athens only had advisory powers and could not formulate policy on behalf of the Greek state. Their "advisory" powers, however, carried the weight of the Protecting governments and ever since the creation of the Greek kingdom the Powers' Legations influenced policy in Greece. The Commission therefore was intended to be used as an instrument of recommending policy to the Greek State which it had to adopt otherwise the Commission's existence was meaningless.

Before the Commission's second meeting on 25 February, the Greek government submitted to Wyse the document he had requested on its first meeting. Ironically the foreign troops in Pireaus were still in Greece two days after the Commission's second meeting. The occupation finally ended on 28 February[61] after the Greek government showed its cooperation and yielded the documents which Wyse requested. The British government appointed Edward Strickland to assist Wyse in the analysis of the Greek financial data submitted to the Commission. Strickland was a financial expert whose role was to act as an advisor to the Commissioners. He could also make recommendations to the host government concerning financial improvements in Greece.[62] Strickland's French colleague was Marquis de Ploeuc who in 1859 was appointed commissioner to investigate Turkey's financial status.[63]

The Commission's first duty was the investigation of the Greek government's report on the perishable national property. A thorough analysis of the National Estates would have followed in order to determine if maximum yield was derived from them. The Commission would then forward its recommendations to the administration at Athens so that it could make more efficient use of the State property. An examination of the nation's tax system, its customs revenues and other probably unexploited resources were to be carefully analyzed in order to open new channels of revenue for the Greek state.[64] Lord Clarendon echoed the same optimism about the Commission's goal as Wyse. The British Foreign Secretary told Trikoupis that Great Britain wished to provide every opportunity for the Hellenic State to improve its finances. Lord Clarendon stressed, however, that to accomplish its task the Commission needed the Greek Ministry's full cooperation.[65]

The Voulgaris administration had little choice but to cooperate with the Commission. One of the first lengthy reports which the government presented to the Commissioners was an expose of the country's economy since 1821. The twenty-four page report was designed to prove to the Powers that Greece made enormous economic progress since her independence. The report pointed out the progress in agriculture during Otho's reign, the construction of new cities and reconstruction of old ones, the country's progress in navigation, and the construction of new ports such as Pireaus. Revenues from Customs increased tremendously as the nation's commerce and navigation flourished. From two million drachmas in import duties in 1835 the government proudly announced that the amount had doubled in 1857. Furthermore, the report tried to impress the Commission by showing that seven hundred thousand stremmata of National Land was sold to private landowners for cultivation since 1821.[66]

The report pointed out the deficiencies of the State's revenue system indicating that not all Greek resources were exploited. Minerals and forestry were two of the major unexplored resources of State revenue but the report maintained that legislation was introduced to remedy these deficiencies. Finally, in order to dissolve charges that Greek revenues made no progress during Otho's reign, the government ascertained that in 1833 the State's revenues, without counting the loan, were 7,950, 000 drachmas, in 1840 they increased to 16,000,000 and in 1856 to 18,000,000. The deficits which were higher than the receipts were justified in view of the regenerated nation whose progress demanded a continuous higher expenditure. Against British allegations that Greek revenues were primarily absorbed by military expenditure the government submitted the following chart outlining each Ministry's expenditure in 1843 and in 1956. It should be noted that the chart did not reflect the total expenditure. The report concluded that based on these expenditures it was clear that the State spent a great deal of its revenues for public works and instruction.

1843

Ministry of Navy. 1,452,465
Ministry of War. 5,282,004
Ministry of the Interior. 1,168,514
Ministry of Foreign Affairs   393,712
Ministry of Public Instruction
    and Worship   547,510
Ministry of Justice.   848,528
Ministry of Finance 3,976,589
TOTAL. 13,669,322

	1856	Difference
Ministry of Navy.	1,599,873	147,408
Ministry of War.	5,494,570	212,566
Ministry of the Interior.	2,404,479	1,235,965
Ministry of Foreign Affairs	564,072	170,360
Ministry of Public Instruction		
and Worship	1,080,024	532,514
Ministry of Justice.	1,447,944	599,416
Ministry of Finance	4,874,464	897,875
TOTAL[67]	17,465,426	3,796,104

The documentation of the above report was misleading for it was designed to dispell Franco-British accusations against the corruption and
mismanagement of Greek finances. It is true that there was some economic
progress in the nation since 1821 but this was certainly to be attributed
to the private economic sector, and not to the government which hindered economic progress. As indicated in the previous chapter, Greek ag.:-
culture did not progress after 1837 due to the government's taxation
system. Navigation did in fact score considerable gains since 1832 but the
goverrnment's own naval force decreased during Otho's reign. The chart
on the following page indicates Greek navigation progress from the outbreak of the Revolution to Otho's exile.

The state, however, made no such progress. In 1842 the navy consisted
of thirty-four ships, in 1851 fourteen and in 1855 eleven vessels manned
by 1,150 at a cost of 1,150,000 drachmas.[69]

Navigation[68]

Year	Ships	Tons
1821	449	52,000
1831	2,685	—
1832	2,941	—
1834	2,745	—
1838	3,269	85,502
1850	4,046	266,221
1853	4,230	247,661
1858	3,920	268,480
1859	3,984	274,075
1860	4,070	263,075
1861	4,153	265,977
1862	4,335	257,318

The administration also concluded in its report that a great deal of the public expenditure was devoted for public instruction during Otho's reign. This was not the case at all. In order to have a clearer understanding of how the Greek government deceived the Commission with its report, it would be necessary to view government expenditure before the occupation and after. The budget of 1854, for example, indicated that 1,780, 733 drachmas was allocated for the Ministry of the Interior and 932,488 drachmas for the Ministry of Public Instruction and Worship. As far as public instruction was concerned Otho and his government did the very minimum to improve education as the table on the following page indicates. It shows the country's public instruction made some progress only after the Franco-British occupation which forced the government to curb its war expenditure. But how can it be claimed that Greece made considerable progress in education during Otho's reign when only 52,860 people received any education in 1860 out of a total population of 1,096,810.

The Commission expected to receive a polished report on Greek finances and economy since the administration wished to avoid severe criticism on its finances from the Powers. Wyse asked for further documentation in April from Ragabes. He requested "a statement of the arrears on the expiration of expenditure of 1855, Table of the situation of the Treasury on the 1st January 1857, accounts of expenditure since 1845, but provisionally those years 1850, 1851, 1852, 1853, 1854, and 1855."[71]

Public Instruction[70]

	1830		1855	
Institutions	Écoles	Etudiantes	Écoles	Etudiantes
Université			1	555
Gymnasium			7	968
Écoles Superiure	39	2,528	80	4,224
Écoles Communales				
de Garçons	71	6,721	357	30,520
Écoles Communales				
de Filles			52	4,753

	1860	
	Écoles	Etudiantes
Institutions	1	602
Gymnasium	8	1,289
Écoles Superiure	87	5,739
Écoles Communales		
de Garçons	598	38,427
Écoles Communales		
de Filles	70	6,803

Ragabes complied with the Commission's request but did not send all the designated data. Wyse also asked for a complete statement on the National property.[72] He wished to have a complete account of government property in each province *(nomos)*, county *(eparchia)* and city *(demos)* and a report which outlined the category of that property. The Ministry of Finance prepared a statement which summarized the National Land portions which the State sold or endowed to various sectors of the population.[73]

On 28 May, Wyse complained to Ragabes that the Greek government withheld information vital to the Commissioner's inquiries. Up to that date the administration had sent the following documents to the Commission.

A statement on the arrears outstanding on 31 December 1856, on the "exercises" anterior to 1849; and on 31 December 1855, of the arrears, on the "exercises" subsequent to that date. Four printed volumes containing the "comptes de gestion" of the years 1845, 1851, 1852, 1853, and the "comptes d'exercices" of 1843,

1844, 1850, 1852. The "compte de gestion" of 1846, 1847, 1849 are still awaiting.[74]

The Commission had requested but not received a number of other documents concerning the budget of 1856, the accounts of the duties from 1845 to 1855, and a statement concerning the Treasury's status on 1 January 1857 which outlined the receipts from taxes and other revenues of the 1857 budget.[75] Wyse and his colleagues had a special interest in the revenues derived from Custom duties because that was the main source of Treasury receipts. The British Minister distrusted Greek officials and suspected that the Custom duties contributed more to the Public Treasury than the administration admitted.

Greek officials refused to comply with the Commission's request concerning the submission of complete data on the National Estates. In June, the acting President of the Commission, W. Cambell Manley, protested to the Greek Foreign Ministry concerning its lack of cooperation.[76] The Greek government's reluctance to submit all the requested documentation to the Commission was due to several factors. First, there was the lack of bureaucratic efficiency.[77] Secondly, the Commission asked for precise land statistics concerning the National property which did not exist. Finally, the King and his Cabinet resented having to produce financial evidence which proved to the Powers what they suspected all along, that Greek finances were in a chaotic state and the government was indeed corrupt. To avoid incriminating itself in such manner the administration deliberately withheld information throughout the Commissions' inquiries.

Seven months after the Commission started its inquiries Edward Strickland and Campbell Manley were dissatisfied with the Greek officials' unwillingness to cooperate. They protested to Ragabes about the delays which the Cabinet caused to the Commission's work, and requested better cooperation from the host government.[78] The Greek Foreign Minister responded that his government wished to cooperate with the Commissioners and assured Campbell Manley that eventually the administration would produce all the documents which Wyse had requested. He explained, however, that a great deal of information concerning the finances for the years 1853 through 1856 was missing and exact information concerning the National lands was nonexistent. Finally, Ragabes reminded the British plenipotentiary that compiling the required documentation demanded extensive labor on the part of Greek officials but he promised nevertheless to hand over the data which the Commission wished to examine.[79]

During the first seven months of the Commission's existence the British Legation played the protagonist role but it enjoyed the French and Russian Legations' approval. It was evident, however, that the British were more serious about the Commission and its purpose than the other two Powers. The Russian Minister at Athens, Count Ozeroff, expressed his appreciation to Ragabes on several occasions for the Greek government's patience, goodwill and cooperation with the Commission's financial inquiries.[80] The British Legation rarely expressed any appreciation to Greek officials for their cooperation with the Commission's inquiries. Furthermore, the British Legation kept much of the information related to Greek finances from the Russian and French representatives. Count Ozeroff formally protested that the British tried to dominate the Commission. He demanded that as an equal representative he wanted to be informed on all issues in regards to Greek finances and about the Commission.s progress and actual position.[81]

Greece relied on Russia as her only true ally of the three Powers to restrain the Commission's excessive powers. The Cabinet feared first that the Commission could become a permanent body in Greece, and second, that it could intervene in the country's domestic affairs and make policies. In December the Tsar assured S. Soutsos, the Greek representative in St. Petersburg, that the Commission was temporary and it would only examine Greek financial matters without interfering in the nation's politics, or disrupt her sovereignty.[82] The Russian Minister at Athens, however, confidentially informed his government in December that the Commission wished to prolong its work indefinitely and to extend its inquiries into every branch of the Administration.[83] Soutsos relayed this information from St. Petersburg to Athens in order to warn his government to take appropriate measures and counter British designs of financial control in Greece.

It was obvious from the British Legation's requests for more detailed information on all aspects of Greek finances and economy, that Great Britain intended to violate the Powers' agreement concerning the Commission's temporary status. In December 1857, Wyse reported to the Foreign Office that Ragabes had not complied with the Commissioners on various occasions. He maintained that all the information which he requested from the Cabinet was vital to the Commission's goal of determining the financial status of Greece.[84]

The burden of data collection fell upon the Ministry of Finance. Wyse pressured Ragabes for information and Ragabes turned to Koumoundouros, Minister of Finance. The Finance Minister could not possibly comply with the Commission's requests for the immense documentation. He explained to the Commissioners that they wanted detailed information which simply was not kept on record. One such example was the Custom Houses. Koumoundouros maintained that:

> The Greek Custom Houses could not give the amount of duty in detail as well as in total cash, specifying the articles on which levied, and the countries from which these came, so as to afford a check in dealing with the returns of each in gross . . . . [85]

Wyse informed Clarendon that many such delays intervened in the past due to neglect, confusion of keeping public accounts, loss of documents and inefficiency of officials. As a result of these factors the Commission had two choices; either to proceed its inquiries with the available documents or to prolong its existence.

Greece suspected that Wyse would use any excuse to prolong the Commission's investigations. At the beginning of 1858 the Ministry of Finance tried as much as it was allowed by Otho and by the availability of information to provide the Commissioners with everything they requested as quickly as possible. In February Koumoundouros submitted to the Ministry of Foreign Affairs a chart of Greek Commerce which outlined the country's imports and exports from 1844 to 1855, with the exception of 1847 and 1848. Koumoundouros also promised to prepare more financial accounts and present them to the Commission as promptly as possible.[86] Ragabes sent the Finance Ministry's report to Wyse[87] and Koumoundouros sent a copy of the same report to Otho.[88] Wyse learned about the report to Otho and asked that Koumoundouros should supply him with a copy.[89] The administration withheld some information on Greek Commercial imports and exports[90] and Wyse protested again that the officials in Athens did not fully comply with the legations' requests. Furthermore, the British Charge d'Affaires protested against the Ministry's reluctance to submit the complete requested information on the Crown property which the Commission asked to receive when it was first established.[91]

On 1 March 1858, Greece defaulted the instalment payments to the Powers on the interest and sinking fund. This forced Count de Plouec to release a premature report to his government which stated that the Commission had already discovered many disorders in Greek finances.[92] The French government presented Plouec's report to that nation's legislative branch for its examination. Ragabes protested against Pouec's action and claimed that the report caused the utmost damage to Greece. He argued that the Commission's inquiries were not completed and the report was not conclusive, therefore it mislead the French government to draw erroneous conclusions about Greek finances.[93] The French government, however, did not need Plouec's report to prejudice its views about Greek finances. Experience of French financial relations with Greece since 1833 taught them that Greek finances were in serious trouble. Ragabes was alarmed, however, by the premature report because he feared that France could support Great Britain if the latter decided on the need for a prolonged or a permanent Commission. The Commission of financial inquiries, in other words, could have been converted into a permanent Commission of financial control.

Many Greeks openly accused the Commission after its establishment as an organ which the Powers used to interfere in Greek foreign and domestic policies.[94] On its second year of investigations the Commission probed deeper into Greek finances. Every aspect of the nation's economy was investigated. Direct and indirect taxes, customs, commerce, business, government and private property, government revenues and expenditures, actual and potential resources. Many government officials, politicians and businessmen felt considerable embarrassment by the Commission's inquiries and the country as a whole felt the tension of the Powers' investigations. In April 1858, Trikoupis complained in London to the Foreign Office that the Financial Commission's inquiries continued needlessly. The Greek ambassador stated that his government supplied all the necessary documentation to the Commission and after a period of over thirteen months of financial investigations the process should have ended. Lord Malmesbury, who replaced Clarendon in April as Foreign Secretary inquired from the British Legation in Athens to report on the Commission's progress its delays.[95]

Wyse wrote to Malmesbury that the delays were due to (a) the lack of information, (b) the great labor hours needed to furnish the documentation and (c) Greek bureaucrats' negligence and unpreparedness for such a task. Ultimately, the British representative concluded, the Ministry at Athens was responsible for the delay.[96] In response to Trikoupis' charge that the Commission probed too deeply into Greek finances and the country's economy, Wyse reminded Malmesbury that the Commission was authorized to investigate the following sectors of Greek finances:

1. The Financial Administration and Receipts from both Direct and Indirect Taxation.
2. The Collection of Taxes
3. Expenditure
4. Resources
5. Remedies and Reforms to be submitted to the Greek government if approved by our respective governments.[97]

By April 15 the Commission had only completed "the first division of the subject" with still four more to examine.[98]

The Ministry at Athens blamed the Commission for deliberately delaying its inquiries and for refusing to designate a date of its termination. Trikoupis asked the Foreign Office to give him an approximate idea of the Commission's closing. Wyse, however, who was the key figure in the Commission and was largely responsible for its delays refused to make any promises which he thought premature. He informed Malmesbury:

> I cannot definitely point out, as I am sure your Lordship will perceive, the precise period at which the Commission is likely to conclude its labors; much must depend on the expendition with which documents are brought under consideration.[99]

Wyse deliberately refused to set the Commission's termination date for he wanted to pressure Greek officials to supply him with every document he requested. The Greeks wanted to terminate the Commission's inquiries because they did not wish any more of their government's financial records revealed to the Powers' representatives.

The Administration in Athens argued that the Commission had cost Greece enormous expenses. Trikoupis complained to Malmesbury that there was considerable paper work involved in supplying the immense financial

information for the Commission's analysis. This process increased the bureaucracy's expenses and the country could not withstand the extraordinary
expenditure.[100] When Lord Malmesbury relayed Trikoupis' protestations
to Wyse the latter bitterly attacked the Greek Ambassador and defended
the Commission's inquiries. He explained that the Financial Commission
was established in February 1857 but its work started in November of the
same year. This was partly due to the absence of its members and some staff
at various times and partly to a consequence of the Greek government's
inability to produce the requested documents. Furthermore, Wyse added,
the Allied Powers agreed with Greece after the Crimean War that they would
withdraw their troops on the condition that a Financial Commission would
be established in Athens to secure an improved financial administration
in that country. At that time the Greeks deceived themselves that the Commission would be an impotent ceremonial organization of the Protecting
Powers. The Greek people and their government did not therefore take the
Commission seriously and hence their expectations that it should be dissolved, Wyse remarked. According to the Treaty of 1832, (Article XII),
however, the Powers had every right to install the Financial Commission
after Greece defaulted her payments on the guaranteed loan. Finally, the
Commission's President concluded:

> We must not only know, what the Greek government receives, and
> how it receives it, but why it does not receive more and what it does
> with what it receives. It is thus only we who can determine the true
> causes which prevent them so long from fulfilling their engage-
> ments.[101]

Wyse reiterated his policy that the Powers had the right of financial control
in Greece because the latter violated the Treaty of 1832, but he did not have
Russian and French wholehearted support for his claims so the Greek government could counter his extremism with the Tsar's diplomatic intervention
in Athens.

In London, Charilaos Trikoupis, son of Spyridon Trikoupis[102] and his
private secretary, continued to protest against Wyse's attempts to prolong
the Commission's work. He complained to Lord Malmesbury that Wyse
was the only member on the Commission responsible for delaying its inquiries. The Foreign Secretary assured him that he would seriously consider

his protestations.[103] After Wyse convinced Malmesbury that the Greek administration caused the delays the British Foreign Secretary assured Trikoupis that Wyse and his two colleagues executed their duty based on the authority of the Treaty of 1832. He further maintained that the Commission needed ample time to do justice to its task. In response the Greek government's allegations that Wyse deliberately delayed the Commission's work which was an enormous expense to the State, Malmesbury stated that the Greek administration was only burdened with limited expenses of "arranging papers already within their reach, a matter which ought long since to have been done in accordance with Greek law...."[104] The most intriguing aspect of Malmesbury's dispatch to Trikoupis was that it revealed the degree of influence Wyse had in British foreign policy in Greece. Of course, the British Legation since 1833 always carried enormous weight in British policy-making in Greece but this case which involved the Commission and the other two guaranteeing governments was extraordinary. The Foreign Office risked its foreign policy on one man whose long adversary relationship with Otho and Greek politicians had prejudiced his views.

Trikoupis realized Wyse's influence in the Foreign Office's policy in Greece and he objected to the Commission's requests for extensive documentation which covered every aspect of Greek finances. He wrote to Malmesbury that his was a tactic used to prolong the Commission's existence which was precisely what Wyse wanted.[105] Trikoupis also protested that his country's sovereignty was in jeopardy by the Commission's prolonged existence and its intensive investigations into the Greek economy and the State's finances.[106] He argued that Article XII of the 1832 treaty did not provide for the establishment of a Financial Commission. According to the Treaty the Powers' representatives had the right to make certain that Greece paid the interest on the guaranteed loan. Nowhere did the Treaty state, however, that the Powers could form a commission which would thoroughly examine Greek finances and investigate the nation's economy. That amounted to nothing less than financial control.

Inspite of Trikoupis' repeated appeals to Malmesbury for the Commission's termination, Wyse and his colleagues continued their efforts uninterrupted. Once they finished their examination of the Financial Administration they requested documentation on forest management, real estate, and a list of the balances of account of the "Grande Livre" (ledgers) from the year 1850 to 1858.[107] In accordance with Wyse's request the Greek

Ministry of Finance submit to the Commission the supplementary and extra-ordinary expenses of the various Ministries from 1856 to 1858.[108] Koumoundouros also accommodated the Commission and provided charts for the Administration's Accounts from 1846 to 1850, and the supplementary and extraordinary credits from 1856 to 1858, and the balance of the "Grande Livre" for the years 1850 to 1854.[109] The Commission examined the nation's mines and minerals, fisheries, saltworks, the agricultural and commercial resources, both actual and potential.[110] Although the Great Powers' Legations "had already from extra or unofficial sources, pretty accurate idea on most of these topics," Wyse insisted that the Greek government should furnish the Commission with the official information. To avoid any further delays the Administration at Athens complied with Wyse's request.[111]

The Ministry of Finance compiled a laborious report which outlined the nation's mines and mineral resources from 1850 to 1856.[112]

Metals and Minerals	Receipts	Expenditures	Difference	
			Surplus	Deficit
Millstone	334,903.21	97,599.50	237,303.71	—
Plaster	47,564.50	3,236.49	44,301.01	—
Coal	23,150.22	34,423.09	—	11,272.87
Thiraikikonia	175,056.96	—	175,056.96	—
Emery	1,494,460.00	206,024.89	1,288,435.11	—
TOTAL	2,075,134.89	341,310.97	1,745,096.79	11,272.87

Koumoundouros also sent a complete report to the Commissioners which listed the country's fisheries and salt-works.[113] The income derived from these resources was insignificant and of no real importance to the Commissioners since they knew approximately what benefit Greece derived from the above resources. Wyse wanted this evidence before the Commission to prove the Greek government's inability to develop the country's potential resources.

After one and a half years since the Commission's establishment the Greeks believed that Wyse and his Russian and French colleagues had more than ample time to complete their unpleasant task. Ragabes informed the British Legation in November that the Administration wanted the financial inquiries to be terminated.[114] Wyse agreed with the Greek Foreign Minister as he informed Malmesbury that the Commission's work had indeed progressed considerably. He felt, however, that there was more material to be reviewed before concluding and still more to be furnished by the Hellenic State. Koumoundouros had not supplied an account of his department's resources and expenditure[115] although he did submit some information concerning the Finance Ministry's expenditures.

In its endless efforts to terminate the Financial Commission the Hellenic government resorted to diplomacy. Trikoupis' appeals to Malmesbury for the Commission's termination failed so the administration in Athens appealed to the French government to relieve Greece of the international financial investigative Committee. The British intelligence sources in Athens learned of the Greek appeals to France and Wyse reported to the Foreign Office:

> . . .in consequence of the representations of the Greek Charge d'Affaires at Paris (M. Roques), urged it would seem by the instructions of M. Ragabe, M. Walewski has strongly urged M. De Montherot (French Minister at Athens) to hasten the termination of the Commission, the grounds being an impression that M. de Plouec had shown disposition to extend his inquiries and observations beyond the strict letter of financial duties, into the domian of politics.[116]

Wyse insisted that the allegation against Plouec was the Greek government's fabrication because Plouec was not charged with political interference in Greek domestic affairs by the Cabinet at Athens, nor was he even aware of any such allegation.

Wyse ascertained that the Greek government invented the charge against M. de Plouec because it was desperate to break the Franco-British solidarity and isolate Britain diplomatically from the other two Powers. The British representative reminded Malmesbury that during the occupation Greece attempted several such diplomatic tactics. Finally, he added, that another reason for the Greek government's diplomatic maneuver in Paris was due to the Commission's latest inquiries into the expenditures of the various Departments which the Ministry resented and was eager "to cut short these examinations, and. . .to close the Commission."[117] There is little doubt that Wyse's assessment of Greek tempermant concerning the Commission was correct. Greece had to use diplomacy as its ultimate weapon against any deeper penetration into its finances by the Powers. Russia could do little to aid Greece for after the Crimean War her diplomatic strength in Greece was undermined by the Allied Powers. The French presented the ideal balance of power in the Protectorate. The influence of France in the Voulgaris administration, however, was minimal and the King entertained Russophile sentiments which made him suspect to Napoleon III's government. So Wyse and Great Britain prevailed because Greece had a weak ally in Russia and Otho had alienated the Francophiles from the government.

Before the Commission drew its final conclusion in May 1859, Wyse made certain that Greece would be robbed of every bit of private and confidential financial data possible. One of the more sensitive areas which the Commission investigated was the finances of the Departments of War and Navy. Wyse insisted that the Commission's work was incomplete unless a series of questions respecting the expenditures in these Departments were answered.[118] At first the Greeks were reluctant to turn over to the Powers' representatives military secret information which the Powers could use against Greece,[119] but finally the will of the mightly prevailed.

In order to avoid severe criticism by the Commission, which could have led to a permanant financial control in Greece by the Powers, the administration selected documentation which exemplified the nation's economic progress. The Ministry of the Interior prepared many such documents comparing the progress of agriculture from the years of the Revolution to the present.[120] The following statistics clearly illustrate the Greek economic progress yet they were quite deceptive.

(A) Raisins. 30,000 stremmata cultivated during the War of Independence; total produce 16 to 18 million litres. In 1857, 160,000 stremmata were under cultivation which produced 80,000,000 litres raisins.

(B) Vineyards. 20,000 to 25,000 stremmata, for a total produce of 5,000,000 okades during the War of Independence. In 1857, 700,000 stremmata produced a total of 140,000,000 okades.

(c0 Orchards. During the War of Independence there were 386,000 productive trees; in 1857 the number increased to 1,500,000 trees.

(D) Olive trees. No statistics for the War of Independence. In 1857, 7,000,000 trees.

(E) Vegetables. In 1857, 7,500,000 stremmata. No statistics for the War of Independence.

(F) Number of Houses. In 1833, there were 94,927 houses in Greece in 1857, 203,605.

(G) Navigation. During the War of Independence Greece had 440 ships for a total tonnage of 52,000. In 1857 there were 4,230 ships which totaled 247,661 tons and employed 27,000 men.[121] In 1858 there were 6,174 sailboats, 731 steamboats in Greek ports. Total tonage for sailboats was 186,494, and for steam boats 363,791. The grand total was 550,285 tons. From 1843 to 1858, 3,586 boats were constructed in Greece for 255,671 tons, occupying a working force of 19,942 men.[122]

It appears from the above documentation that Greece made a great deal of economic progress during Otho's reign. Several factors must be taken into consideration, however, before reaching any hasty conclusions. First, the comparisons above are deceptive because the government showed the nation's economic progress and tried to be credited for the achievements of the private economic sector. The government had little to do with the increase in agricultural production or the increases in housing and navigation. These were achievements of the people, not of King Otho and the administration. Secondly, the comparisons were deceptive because during the War of Independence there was economic stagnation and in most cases regress. Finally, the statistics did not reflect the actual economic conditions of Greece because the Ministry of the Interior specifically selected those sectors of the economy which had shown progress. To obtain a fair representation of Greek economic progress during Otho's reign it is important to analyze all sectors of the economy and not just those who showed significant progress. The Administration, however, did not care about a fair representation of the Greek economy, it only wished to impress the Commission with the nation's progress.

Wyse received the report from the Ministry of the Interior[123] but had serious reservations about the report's validity. He believed that many statements in the report were questionable, especially those concerning Greek resources and new financial prospects. He wrote to Malmesbury:

> . . . the facts and conclusions to which we had arrived in the course
> of our previous investigations, contributed to shake our confidence
> in the accuracy or frankness of communications, and to diminish the

weight we might have been disposed to attach to this, in particular.[124]

He also stated that neither he nor the Commission were authorized to force the truth out of the administration. There was no way therefore that the documentation which Greece submitted to the Commission could be verified.

In August 1858, Wyse and his fellow Commissioners requested statements concerning Greek commercial resources. Six months passed and Ragabes had not complied with the Commission's request. In February 1859, Wyse asked the Foreign Ministry to forward a report to the Commission concerning the country's commercial activity during the decade of the 1850s.[125] The Foreign Minister wished to avoid any further confrontations with Wyse so in March 1859 he sent the report.[126] This was the most detailed of all the documents which the Cabinet furnished the Commission. It enumerated the nation's major imports and exports from 1851 to 1857. Like the previous reports on Greek economic progress the March Report was also clearly prejudiced in so far as it was selective.

Exports[127]

Year	Cocoon	Wine	Salt
1851	—	714,391 dr.	—
1852	1,999,970 dr.	1,022,545 dr.	—
1853	1,774,063 dr.	1,274,046 dr.	105,000 okades
1854	1,353,018 dr.	711,694 dr.	178,188 okades
1855	1,884,460 dr.	890,815 dr.	96,000 okades
1856	1,814,499 dr.	873,728 dr.	2,555,162 okades
1857	1,493,934 dr.	956,982 dr.	1,062,044 okades

Year	Leather	Tobacco	Figs
1851	—	—	—
1852	103,537 dr.	82,521 dr.	700,175 dr.
1853	181,184 dr.	257,689 dr.	919,126 dr.
1854	175,450 dr.	159,995 dr.	682,479 dr.
1855	240,000 dr.	194,457 dr.	1,398,710 dr.
1856	163,637 dr.	336,267 dr.	1,236,309 dr.
1857	355,152 dr.	783,499 dr.	737,743 dr.

Exports (continued)

Year	Cereals	Oil	Corinth Raisins	
			litres	Valeur
1851	–	236,582 dr.	57,662,756	8,359,196
1852	389,066 dr.	47,864 dr.	16,492,266	2,844,058
1853	548,528 dr.	22,375 dr.	16,662,244	–
1854	155,732 dr.	191,429 dr.	10,745,472	–
1855	–	292,704 dr.	11,272,660	1,687,183
1856	747,088 dr.	244,167 dr.	–	16,471,620
1857	655,335 dr.	56,593 dr.	–	13,474,628

Imports

Year	Leather	Cereals	Oil
1851	–	–	155,457 dr.
1852	953,077 dr.	7,892,295 dr.	705,663 dr.
1853	896,102 dr.	2,749,394 dr.	330,373 dr.
1854	939,583 dr.	5,621,839 dr.	202,374 dr.
1855	500,000 dr.	6,000,000 dr.	71,923 dr.
1856	691,069 dr.	5,464,684 dr.	212,217 dr.
1857	1,718,074 dr.	3,800,527 dr.	1,035,569 dr.

The above report relfected Greek economic progress in the 1850s and it emphasized the nation's exports. Like other Greek government reports which were designed to impress the Commission with the country's progress the above was no exception. On the basis of that report's statistics, Greece seemed to have made considerable economic progress. When the country's total trade is considered, however, Greece suffered an enormous trade deficit during the last ten years of Otho's reign. Imports from 1851 to 1864 totaled 529,626,138 drachmas, and exports for the same period totaled 282,006,397 drachmas.[128]

The trade statistics were among the last ones which the Greek government submitted to the Commission. The inquiries ended after twenty-five months and the Commission was ready to review all the financial data available and draw its conclusions. As far as Wyse was concerned the Greek government had not cooperated wholeheartedly with him and his colleagues. As far as the Greek officials were concerned the Commission had exceeded its authority by investigating confidential financial data. It was certain, however, that the Powers received privileged information which they wanted in order to determine why Greece defaulted her instalment payments. The very existence of the Commission constituted a violation of the Treaty of 1832 but so did the Greek government's failure to meet its financial obligations to the Protecting Powers.

C. Conclusions

In March 1859 the Commissioners requested the Greek Ministers of Finance and Foreign Affairs to sit in a special session with the Commission in order to cross examine their observations concerning Greece's financial status. On the first meeting between the Greek Ministers and the Powers' representatives, Koumoundouros agreed with the Commission's general conclusions concerning the lack of Greek financial documentation and he also agreed to continue his participation in more sessions with the Commissioners.[129]

In the beginning of May, Wyse informed the Foreign Office that the Commission's work was drawing to a close. The three representatives agreed before they submitted an official final report to their respective governments, first, to state the object and nature of the Financial Commission, second, to outline the length of this organization, and finally, to explain the program presented on the subjects and order of inquiries. They agreed that the order of topics which the Commission should follow should be Administration, Receipts, Collection, Resources, Expenditure, Debt and Reforms.[130] Before the Commissioners drew the final observations, Ragabes feared that Wyse and his colleagues formulated an erroneous impression about the state of Greek finances based on the Greek government's optimistic reports which emphasized the nation's progress. He requested, therefore, a few days before the Commission's closing to produce documentation from the Ministry of the Interior which outlined the necessities for road construction, other vital public works and a list of the country's domestic debt.[131] Wyse replied that he took these factors into consideration but pointed out to Ragabes that public works were funded by local taxes, tolls, and by public contributions.[132] Since the Foreign Minister failed to convince the British Charge d'Affaires about the nation's needs for internal development, the Administration hoped that France and Russia would restrain Wyse from imposing large instalment payments on Greece.

Russia did in fact come to Otho's rescue once again and attempted her utmost to minimize the Greek government's financial burden by opposing Wyse's severe measures against Greece. Wyse and Montherot proposed a plan which gave to the Legislative Branch of the Greek government more financial powers than to the Cabinet. This measure was strictly designed to deprive the King, who controlled the Cabinet, from exercising dominant authority in the nation's financial affairs. Ozeroff opposed this measure because he claimed, it was an attempt on the Powers' part to interfere directly into Greek institutions. In a final settlement the Western Powers' representatives compromised with Ozeroff. They agreed to state in their final report that the Chamber of Deputies had neglected its duties and failed to check and correct the country's financial abusses.[133]

The next issue on which Russia acted as the moderate force in the Commission to Greece's benefit was about the instalment payments for the loan. Wyse proposed at first that Greece could afford and should pay two million drachmas annually to the three Powers. Ozeroff, and surprisingly, Montherot were against Wyse's proposal. The French and the Russian representatives argued that such an enormous annual sum would incapacitate Greece totally and the Powers could have no benefit from such an outcome. Wyse then asked his colleagues to agree to the sum of one and a half million, but they refused to concur with the British Minister once again and he had to compromise with Ozeroff's and Montherot's plan. The three representatives finally decided to set the annual sum at nine hundred thousand francs or one million drachmas. Wyse was not content with the compromise but he had little choice. He wrote to Malmesbury about the proposed payment plan:

> This sum of 900,000 francs tho much below the annual payment due under the stipulations of the Convention, is yet the triple of that Mr. Ragabe offered . . . . It is also limited to the first payment only. The next paragraph proposes to provide for a gradual increase.[134]

The "gradual increase" was not determined by the Commission but was to be based upon the State's increased revenues. Ozeroff wanted a paragraph inserted in the final report which stated that in the interest of Greek public works the Powers would waiver their charge on the interest and sinking fund. Wyse naturally objected and claimed that Greece used the excuse of "in the interests of public works" frequently in order to avoid her payments to the Powers. The paragraph was omitted.

Among the most serious criticisms which the Commission made about Greek finances or the lack of them were the following. There was an increase of Forest Agents from 146 in 1845 to 200 in 1859 without any improvements in forestry. The Commission maintained that this was one case of bureaucratic expansionism which was fruitless and burdensome to the Public Treasury. In 1849 it cost the government 50,000 francs to service the forests; it spent 111,000 francs ten years later.[135] Furthermore, the Commission charged that no one knew the forests' boundaries, and that there was widespread corruption among forestry officials, mismanagement and disorganization at all levels. These elements the report charged contributed to an overall inefficient bureaucracy.[136]

According to the Commissioners there was also mismanagement of Custom Houses which was one of the most important revenue sources for the Public Treasury. A correction of this problem the Commission suggested would produce increased receipts for the government. The Bavarian loan of four million drachmas was not paid to King Ludwig and decisive measures should have been adopted to liquidate it. The same held true for the debt to the bondholders of the 1824 and 1825 loans. Instead of repaying its debts the Greek government wasted the Public funds the report charged. The expenditure for four prisons at Syra, Kalamata, Sparta and Messolongi, for example, was four hundred thousand drachmas and it should have been avoided, Wyse maintained. The construction of a "Palace of Justice" which cost four hundred thousand drachmas the British representatives considered an extravagant expense. The above mentioned funds should have been applied for repayment of the Greek foreign debt. Finally, the Commission stated that the Justice Department budget in 1843 was 848,000 drachmas, but in 1857 it escalated to 1,516,000 representing an increase of 668,000 drachmas. The increase was unjustifiable and it represented wasteful spending because there was little progress in that Department.

The most wasteful spending according to the Commission took place in the Department of Navy. In 1843 the Navy's expenditure amounted to 1,384,000 drachmas; in the 1860 budget the Navy's expenditure was

2,299,000 drachmas. The increase of expenditure in seventeen years was 915,000 drachmas. During the same period the government spent 1,920, 000 drachmas for the construction of a transport vessel and the Navy's extraordinary expenses amounted to 1,384,000 drachmas. All of these expenses for the kingdom of only a million people were considered wasteful. What was particularly wasteful according to the Commission's findings were the costs for construction and maintance of ships, considering there was relatively little improvement in the Greek navy during Otho's reign.

Year	Construction of Ships	Maintenance of Ships and Ports[137]
1850	200,000.00 dr.	280,870.00 dr.
1851	200,000.00 dr.	179,999.72 dr.
1852	200,000.00 dr.	158,265.06 dr.
1853	—	141,000.00 dr.
1854	—	141,000.00 dr.
1855	—	195,000.00 dr.
1856	455,000.00 dr.	150,000.00 dr.
1857	—	—
1858	—	393,000.00 dr.
1859	575,000.00 dr.	147,000.00 dr.
1860	370,000.00 dr.	197,000.00 dr.

Extraordinary expenses for the War Department were 2,240 drachmas. These funds were spent for construction of barracks at Athens, with an additional 50,000 for repair of barracks on the frontiers, and 50,000 for other military buildings and barracks throughout Greece. All of this expenditure Wyse maintained was wasteful.

The Commission also criticized the Department of the Interior for abusing government revenues. In 1843 credit taken for construction repairs of roads amounted to 234,325 drachmas, 35,672 expended and 198,653 unexpended. In 1855 credits taken for the same were 189,800, with 121,669 expended and 67,831 unexpended. The budget of 1860 demanded 100,000 for road repairs, 378,000 for bridge and road construction. The Department of the Interior budget for 1843 was 1,061, 000, for 1857 3,585,000 and for 1860, 2,880,000 drachmas.[138] The

Commission concluded that there were widespread abuses in the government, both in the sector of collection and of expenditure.

Ragabes, Koumoundouros and other ministers labored for two years since the Commission's establishment to prove that there was a great deal of economic progress during Otho's reign. There was no mention in the Commission's final report, however, of Greek economic progress only of financial abuses during the Othonian era. The Commission ignored the Government's statistics on the private economic sector because they were partial, incomplete and irrelevant to its ultimate goal.

The Commission's official report on their findings and recommendations was signed on 12/24 May 1859, and it reflected the summarized observations of T. Wyse, A. Ozeroff and Charles de Montherot. Below are listed a few of the major observations upon which the Commissioners agreed.

> That the national domain, which is neithter marked out nor known, is being constantly lessened by encroachments; That the communal funds, and the use which is made of them, have been ignored up to the present time by the State thus escaping its supervision, although it was by law entrusted with the guardianship of the communes, whose prosperity is the principal element of the general prosperity of the nation; . . . That the land tax, in particular, gives rise to abuses prejudicial to the Treasury, and that this tax impedes the development of agriculture, which is the principal resource of Greece; That the agents charged with the administration, as well as with the collection, of the public treasure, also escape supervision, which is, however, clearly directed in the Legislation; . . . Seeing that the "Ministres Ordonnateurs" of the expenditure had not rendered up to the present time any account; That the Ministers of Finance had scarcely ever, since the year 1845, verified either the resources of the public Treasury, or the use which had been made of them, by the accounts which the law ordered them to publish, since, if the accounts of 1850, 1851, and 1852, had been made out at the time of the appointment of the Commission, the account of 1850 only had been submitted to the Chambers, and no financial law had been passed; Seeing that the Court of Accounts has not

established, by the declarations of conformity, and by the reports which it is bound to publish, that the administration is regular, and that the accounts of the Ministers are such as they ought to be; Seeing that the Chambers have not remedied this state of things, since, in fact, the Legislative control has been no more exercised than the judicial control; And that, therefore, the accounts produced by the Administration do not offer all the legal guarantees of exactitude and authenticity;—In Short: That the administration of finance has not been regulated with the necessary order; That the efforts of the different agents have not had for their result, as often as they should, the serious application of the laws; That the publicity and the control of the acts of the Administration, which are the guarantees of the country and of the protecting Powers, do not, in fact, exist.[139]

The above criticisms were clearly designed to minimize Otho's power in financial State affairs and to increase the politicians' role in financial policy. The Powers could exert much influence in Greek State affairs through the politicians and would not have to rely on Court's favoritism.

In regard to the guaranteed loan the Commission reported the following based on the availability of Greek financial documents. The Treasury's resources increased steadily during Otho's reign but so did the expenditure while Greece failed to make any payments on her foreign debt. As a result of her default Greece did not have credit standing among European nations.[140] In order to correct the existing financial condition Greece had to alter her practices in government according to the Commission. The Commissioners recommended that "to the imperious necessity of ensuring publicity to the acts of the Administration, and their control by the judicial and legislative powers created by special laws and by the Constitution." This recommendation was designed to create a balance of power in the government again stripping away Otho's dominant influence in the Administration.

In order to justify the Commission's severe criticisms of the Greek government and its finances, Wyse sent a special dispatch to the Foreign Office which outlined the reasoning behind the conclusions which he and his colleagues reached. He wrote that Greece made two payments to Great

Britain since 1843, one in 1847 and the other in 1848, for the total sum of 793,552 francs. Since 1848 Greek revenues increased considerably but the government did not make any more payments to the Powers. The country's expenditure, Wyse contended, was wasteful and destructive before the Crimean War when Greece engaged in an undeclared war against Turkey. The Commissioners' recommendations were designed to limit the Public Treasury's wasteful expenses and to create a better government in Athens. Finally, Wyse concluded that Great Britain should be credited with the Financial Commission's establishment but he added that the other Powers' representatives cooperated and all three Legations at Athens of France, Russia and England acted in unison.[141]

Wyse was proud that he was the one to propose the Commission's establishment, to impose financial inquiries and limitations upon Greece and to criticize and recommend changes in the Greek government. Russia did not wish for a Commission and France only agreed to it because of Otho's Russophile policies. Throughout the Commission's existence Ozeroff and Montherot opposed Wyse's extremist financial measures against Greece. The British Legation at Athens wanted to impose a permanent Financial Commission in Greece and to have total financial control in that nation but the French and Russian representatives opposed such measures. Wyse was able, however, to impose partial financial control in Greece through the Commission. One of the paragraphs in the Commission's final report allowed the Powers to examine Greek budgets.

> For this purpose, at the periods fixed by the laws for the presentation of the Budgets, the production of accounts by the Ministers, the publication of the General Report of the Court of Accounts and of its declarations of conformity, and the promulgation of the Law of Accounts, printed copies of these documents, in sufficient numbers, shall be furnished to the Legations of England, France and Russia.[142]

The Powers' Legations had the right to review Greek budgets and strongly advise for or against allocation of funds. This amounted to partial financial control or to put it mildly, "influence" in Greek financial affairs.

Finally, the Commission's final report set the annual instalment payment for Greece at 900,000 francs. The Greek officials did not know that the Powers had agreed on this amount and no one in the government was briefed about the Commissioners' report before they submitted it to their respective governments. The Commission kept the Greek government ignored of its final report until October 1859, five months after its completion. Roques confidentially informed the Ministry of Foreign Affairs in June that the Commissioners drew up its final report and decided that the annual instalment payment which Greece should pay after 1859 was 900,000 francs. Walewski informed the Greek Charge d'Affaires at Paris about the report and the later relayed this information to Ragabes.[143]

Roques protested to the French Foreign Minister against the Commission's decision to impose a large annual instalment upon Greece. He argued that the Greek Public Treasury could not afford 900,000 francs in annual payments allocated for the foreign debt. He warned that the consequences of such a large payment would be financial chaos in the nation.[144] Walewski responded that the Powers supported the Commission's decision not so much for financial reasons but for political. The British and the French governments were concerned with brigandage in Greece which the Court secretly supported since Kolettes' government. Furthermore, the Western Powers opposed Otho's Russophile policy and anti-Turkish attitude. Walewski pointed out to Roque that there was considerable anti-Western propaganda in the Greek press and on several occasions there were demonstrations by students in Athens against England and France.[145] All these factors convinced the Foreign Office and Walewski to impose high instalment payments upon Greece so that her government would change its existing anti-Western policies.

Ragabes requested from the French government a complete copy of the Commission's final report and ordered the Greek representatives in London and St. Petersburg to submit the same request to their respective host governments.[146] The Powers naturally declined to comply with Ragabes' request because the representatives in Athens were not ready to present their report to the Greek government. The Greek press which had criticized the Commission on several occasions during its sessions since 1857 printed a story in July 1859 to embarrass it and create public excitement against it for its persistent secrecy. The story which appeared in the press claimed that two officials were sent to Athens by foreign Powers to examine the Commission's archives and to underscore its independence.[147] This was a fabricated story which did not motivate Wyse and his colleagues to give in to Greek pressure for submitting the final report.

The Administration in Athens anxiously awaited the Commission's report and while it waited it wished the Protecting Powers to know the Greek government's attitude on the Commission's secrecy and its findings. In a confidential dispatch addressed to the Greek representatives at St. Petersburg, Paris and London, Ragabes condemned the Commissioners at Athens for their refusal to publicize their observations.[148] He also criticized their decision to impose 900,000 francs annual instalment payment on Greece without consulting Greek officials before reaching that decision. Ragabes informed Roque, Trikoupis and Zographos that Greece would have to postpone her vital financial needs in order to satisfy the Commission's outrageous financial demands.[149]

The reason that the Powers' Legations decided against publicizing their observations on Greek finances was because they awaited receipt of their report with comments from their respective governments. As Wyse wrote to Russell, "in the meantime it would be necessary, that the most entire secrecy and reserve should be maintained."[150] The Commission finally submitted its report to the Greek government on 21 October.[151] Ozeroff wrote to the new Foreign Minister, G. Koundouriotes, that the Protecting Powers unanimously, approved the final report and supported the Commissioners' conclusions without reservations. The Russian Minister further stated that Greece had to pay an annual sum of 900,000 francs to the Powers for the interest and sinking fund on the guaranteed loan. Finally, he expressed on behalf of Russia, France and Great Britain, the best intentions and wishes for Greek economic progress and assured Koundouriotes that Russia respected the "independence and dignity of the Hellenic government."[152] Wyse followed his Russian colleague's example and sent a similar dispatch to the Greek Foreign Minister along with the Commission's report. He outlined the Commission's purpose, its investigations and its conclusions. He assured Koundouriotes that it was all executed for the general interest of Greece.[153]

In spite of the Powers' Ministers professed good intentions toward Greece, the country, the government and most important of all the King, resented the Commission and its insulting investigations and observations of Greek finances. On 29 October 1859, Otho delivered the following address to the Chamber of Deputies which expressed his resentment toward the Financial Commission's final report.

> It is known, that my government, has tried to fulfill the nation's obligations toward the three Protecting Powers; it had suggested to them that the matter of the loan be settled permanently according to the country's resources. They (the Powers) responded presently by 900,000 francs as the annual payment, assured that this sum would not interpose an obstacle to the course and regular development to the public service. My government would like to request from you the proper trust, and would like to repeat the negoation for the permanent arrangement concerning the matter of the loan, necessarily needed for the settlement of our Finances and the stability of the public trust.[154]

After Otho's official dissapproval of the Commission's conclusions, the Administration did not acknowledge receipt of the final report and refused to make any comments on it to the Powers' representatives at Athens. Ozeroff and his French colleague were not eager for the Government's prompt response but Wyse held several meetings with Koundouriotes and urged him to give serious consideration to the report and avoid any further delays.[155] The British Charge d'Affaires feared the Greek response to the Commission's findings and resolutions and informed Plouec that the Greek monarch would only agree to set the annual instalment charges at a minimum of 600,000 francs.

Otho's government had failed to neutralize Britain's diplomatic supremacy at Athens since 1857 and Greece had little choice but to abide by the Powers' will. Unable to reduce the instalment payments to 600,000 francs, the Administration attempted to delay the date of the first instalment. The Powers wanted the payment to commence at the end of 1859. The Greeks argued that they could not possibly meet that deadline because the 1861 budget was on the floor before the Chamber of Deputies in November and the Cabinet needed time to adopt the annual instalments into the budget. The Greek government also argued that 900,000 francs was the maximum sum which the Treasury could withstand and the Cabinet did not plan to increase the instalment payments as the nation's resources augmented for fear of plunging the country into financial chaos.[156] The Powers were not as concerned about the increased payments, however, as they were about the designated annual sum which Greece agreed to discharge beginning in 1860.

Finally, the Greek Court and Ministry requested the Foreign Office to withhold publication of the Commission's final report in Greece for they feared that it would cause considerable embarrasment for all parties concerned.[157] The British agreed to that request for they wished also to avoid social disturbances in Greece and further anti-British sentiments as a result of the Powers' interference in Greek financial affairs. The Commission's most damaging work, however, was its refusal to publicize its findings on Greek finances because the people remained ignorant of their government's abuses, corruption and lack of effective leadership. The report should have been published so that the people could see their government's incompetence and the Powers' interventionist policy in Greece.

D. Otho's Exile and the Great Powers

Otho's last two years as Greek monarch were the most turbulant of his entire reign. Brigandage activities escalated and social unrest spread rapidly throughout major cities. The domestic disturbances naturally effected the country's finances. In December 1859, the Administration asked Lord Russell, the British foreign secretary, for an extension on the instalment payment. Great Britain declined to grant any further extensions to the government and the other two Powers followed her example.

The Greek Minister of Finance introduced a bill in the Chamber of Deputies by which the budget of 1860 included 900,000 francs for the Powers.[158] In London Trikoupis opposed the prompt payment to the Powers. He advised the Greek Foreign Minister not to yield to the Powers' pressure and to postpone any payments to them until after they signed the agreement concerning the Commission's instalment plan. Furthermore, Trikoupis insisted that the Administration at Athens should inform the Protecting Powers that since Greece was forced to discharge a high annual payment to the Powers, it could not possibly afford to liquidate her financial obligations to the bondholders.[159] This of course was a delaying tactic but it could not possibly be effective.

The Chamber of Deputies did not delay passage of the Foreign Minister's bill because most Greek politicians realized the consequences which Greece would confront if it continued to default her instalment payment for the guaranteed loan. On 21 June 1860, Koundouriotes informed the Greek plenipotentiaries in London, Paris and St. Petersburg, to assure the guaranteeing governments that Greece would place at their disposal the instalment payment as designated by the Financial Commission.[160] Koundouriotes forwarded a thirty-three page report to the Greek representatives at St. Petersburg, Paris and London in which he criticized the Commission's inquiries and conclusions. He ascertained that the Commission interfered with Greek internal affairs and thus violated the 1832 Treaty. He reminded the three representatives who served at the capitals of the Great Powers that Greece contracted a loan of 60,000,000 francs, but the Powers gave 11,220,598 of that to the Ottoman empire, 1,215,947 to Russia, 333,333 to France, 341,333 to M. Eynard for service charges on a former Greek loan and finally 14,167,282 remained for the nation.[161]

The remaining sum was spent for the Ministry of War, the military, the establishment of the Regency and what was left was absorbed by the interest and sinking fund charges. Greece had nothing left, Koundouriotes concluded, for its Public Treasury. When the Powers insisted that their Protectorate should discharge its financial obligations to them the Administration in Athens could not carry out their requests. In 1847 and 1848 Greece faced brigandage activity which caused social revolts throught Greece The financial consequences of those two years were enormous budget deficits which continued after 1848. In 1850 Great Britain blockaded Pireaus and the country's commerce and navigation suffered considerably. In 1851 and 1852 the nation suffered agricultural disasters, especially in Corinth which produced the finest currants in Greece.[162] All these factors contributed to economic and financial regress in the nation but the Powers failed to take them into consideration.

In 1856, the Western powers requested payment on the interest and sinking fund but Greece was under occupation since May 1854, and could not afford to satisfy the Powers' financial demands. France and Great Britain then decided to install a Financial Commission in Athens which investigated the nation's economy and finances. The Commission's purpose was to make Greece financially more responsible and responsive to her foreign debts. On 24 October 1856, Lord Clarendon assured Trikoupis that a Greek representative would be included in the Commission. The French government concured with Britain's decision on that issue and Prince Gorchakoff insisted that Greece should be represented in the Financial Commission. Ultimately, however, the Powers decided against that proposal and the Greek government did not have the opportunity to participate in the Commission's inquiries and conclusions.[163]

Koundouriotes criticized the Commission's final report and claimed that the Commissioners and their assistants did not have a clear understanding of the National Estates issue and its distribution to the people. The Foreign Minister also criticized the Commission for accusing the Greek government of financial mismanagement and he charged that Wyse and his colleagues in Athens did not realize that the government received less actual revenues than the budget estimates and the recorded receipts in the accounts receivable indicated. Koundouriotes included the following chart which listed confirmed revenues, collected revenues and arrears from 1843 to 1856.

Year	Confirmed Receipts	Collected Receipts	Arrears at the end of the fiscal year[164]
1843	15,103,243.90	12,309,219.55	2,794,024.35
1844	12,997,399.18	10,383,050.36	2,614,348.82
1845	13,650,042.72	10,896,626.53	2,753,416.19
1846	15,988,805.29	12,512,305.84	3,476,499.45
1847	14,774,687.73	11,148,335.38	3,626,352.35
1848	16,074,320.79	12,886,666.59	3,187,654.20
1849	17,805,693.94	14,325,086.81	3,480,607.13
1850	17,639,343.18	14,675,951.46	2,963,391.72
1851	17,674,200.07	14,283,341.93	3,391,858.14
1852	17,980,495.92	14,519,091.04	3,461,404.88
1853	18,661,339.61	15,267,418.01	3,393,921.60
1854	19,930,435.23	16,413,559.34	3,516,875.89
1855	21,181,420.78	18,303,061.84	2,878,358.94
1856	22,403,450.79	20,151,805.50	2,251,645.29

The Commission in its final report accused the Administration for failing to publish its revenues and expenditure. This was a false accusation and

Koundouriotes proved it by presenting a chart which listed the exact dates that the government published its accounts on receipts and expenditures from 1844 until 1857.[165]

Against the Commission's criticism that the Greek Legislators did not actively participate in the government's financial decisions, the Greek Foreign Minister argued that the Chamber of Deputies exercised a great deal of control in the budget. The Deputies had the right of approval or dissapproval of budgets, an element which the Commission totally ignored. Finally, Koundouriotes criticized the Commissioners and their governments for imposing annual instalment payments which were ill founded and ignored Greek economic realities. The annual sum of 900,000 francs for the interest and sinking fund was excessively high and unrealistic in view of the nation's resources. The Powers and the Commission were even more unrealistic to expect the government to increase its instalments as the public revenues increased. Koundouriotes maintained that as the nation's revenues increased so did its expenses. After all, he ascertained, the Commissioners verified that fact. Furthermore, Greece was a young developing nation which augmented its expenditure in order to progress. Public works, State services and education demanded expansion and naturally abosrbed increasing revenues.[166]

Koundouriotes advised Trikoupis, Roques and Zographos to give copies of his dispatch to the guaranteeing governments so that they would know the Greek official position on the Financial Commission. He also asked the three representatives to request from the Great Powers on behalf of the Greek government to divide the annual instalment payment into two bi-annual payments, one due in January and the other in September.[167] The Powers' representatives at Athens reacted angerly to Koundouriotes' stand on the Commission. They resented the Foreign Minister's remarks about the Commission's investigations and observations of Greek finances and they dissapproved of his direct appeal to the guaranteeing governments. They unanimously agreed that Koundouriotes should have sent his government's long awaited remarks on the Commission to the Powers' Legations at Athens directly and not to the Greek ambassadors in France, Russia and Great Britain.[168] Koundouriotes did not address his dispatch to the Powers' Legations in the Greek capital because they would have prejudiced his report with their own preliminary comments as they did so frequently throughout Otho's reign.

Trikoupis, Roques and Soutzos submitted copies of their government's remarks on the Commission to the Protecting Powers.[169] Baron E.P. Brunoff, a Russian senior diplomat, commented after he reviewed Koundouriotes' remarks that it was Great Britain which was determined to examine the Greek finances and not Russia. He assured the Greek Charge d'Affaires at St. Petersburg that the Powers did not wish to impose large annual instalments on Greece and see the government in Athens suffer financially and the nation fall into chaos.[170] Brunoff's sympathic comments about Greece were a sign that Otho still relied on the Tsar's government for diplomatic support. The Russian diplomat's insinuation that Great Britain desired to examine the Greek finances reinforced the Greek government's belief that the Foreign Office had designs of British financial control in Greece.

Koundouriotes addressed a special dispatch to the British Minister at Athens, William Cornwallis Eliot which reiterated the Administration's disapproval of the Commission's report, and of Wyse's role in Greek affairs. The Foreign Minister wrote:

> The communication dated the 20th of October 1859 which the Right Honorable Sir Thomas Wyse did the honor to address to me, inviting the Hellenic government in the name of Her Majesty the Queen of Great Britain, to contribute to the settlement of the loan of sixty millions by a yearly payment of 900,000 francs, has been taken into serious consideration. The Government of the King, while they consider that this demand is far removed from the proposals they had spontaneously submitted in 1856 to the three guaranteeing Powers, and disproportionate to their wants and their resources, has never-the-less determined to carry it out, by imposing on themselves more than one sacrifice, and confining the expenses of the State to what is strictly necessary.[171]

The above dispatch from Koundouriotes to the British Legation was a last effort of protect against the large instalment payments imposed on Greece by the Powers, and a final appeal to Britain which asked for her leniency toward Greece.

British officials, however, were just as discontent with repeated Greek defaults, Greek Russophilism and anti-British attitudes as the Greeks were with Britain's continuous efforts to interfere in the Protectorate's domestic politics and finances. The Lord Commissioners of the British Treasury Chambers criticized the government in Athens for its irresponsible financial conduct toward Great Britain. After the Treasury Chambers received the Commission's final report they expressed their discontent with the Commissioners for they did not impose stricter financial measures on Greece in order to secure payment of the instalment charges. The Treasury Chambers addressed the following remarks to the Foreign Office on the issue:

> Assuming the annual liability of this country to be one third of the whole payments for interest and sinking fund, 900,000 francs a year would amount to about one quarter of the total amount to be provided for the service. The Commissioners do not furnish any data for the conclusion at which they have arrived in this matter; nor have my Lords received from the Secretary of State for Foreign Affairs any proposition for giving effect to the engagement suggested.[172]

The Lords Commissioners of the Treasury Chambers requested the Foreign Office to make proper arrangements in order to avoid further financial complications with Greece.

Britain's determination to force the Greek government into a more responsible financial position was countered by Russia's diplomatic support for Otho's government. The Tsar's government continued to support Greece after the Commission's dissolution and it acted as the moderating force among the three Powers. There were two issues in regards to the instalments which Greece and the Powers had not settled. The first involved the clause in the Commission's final report which stated that as Greek revenues increased the instalment payments also should increase. Great Britain wanted the increase to take effect every five years. France was more moderate and allowed for a ten year period to give Greece ample time for financial recovery. Russia maintained that no dates should be set, but simply asked the Greek government to increase the instalments payments as the State's revenues increased.[173] Prince Gorchakoff also accepted the Koundouriotes proposal concerning the breakdown of the annual instalment payment into two biannual payments and thus set a precedent for the Western Powers to follow.[174]

In August 1861, Napier the British ambassador at St. Petersburg, misinformed Gorchakoff that according to the Commission's report the Greek annual instalments were 900,000 francs to each Power. The Russian Foreign Minister appealed to France and Great Britain immediately not to enforce such high payments on the poor nation. Napier wrote to the Foreign Office about Gorchakoff's reaction:

> He suggested that as the country would be exhausted by so great
> an export of specie, the sum thus summarized should not be
> submitted to the guaranteeing governments at all, but should
> be expended on profitable public works in Greece.[175]

Napier later gave Gorchakoff the correct figure which Greece was asked to pay by the Commission and the Russian Foreign Minister concurred. The Russian government's attitude, however, concerning the Greek foreign debt differed entirely from that of the Western Powers. Russian enjoyed political influence in Greece and allowed Otho's government to suspend payments for the interest on the loan. The French and British governments wanted to minimize the Tsar's influence in Athens so they insisted on prompt and large instalment payments.

In London Trikoupis labored perpetually to convince the Western Powers to follow Russia's example in allowing the Greek government the privilege of making its own decision when to increase the instalments.[176] Trikoupis argued that the Powers reserved the right of ordering Greece to increase her payments on the interest when they desired. This reservation constituted a clear violation of Greek sovereignty and it was an act of direct foreign interference into Greek internal affairs. The guaranteeing governments' power to allocate Greek public revenues deprived Greece of its Treasury's control and amounted to financial control by the Powers. Trikoupis ascertained that the British government which acted according to Wyse's advice on Greek affairs, was the only Power which insisted on the guaranteeing governments' reservation to order Greece when it should increase her instalment payments.[177]

The Greek Charge d'Affaires in London did not convince the Foreign Office to soften its attitude on that issue so he attempted to modify British policy in Greece by using a different diplomatic tactic. Acting on the Greek Foreign Ministry's orders, Trikoupis suggested to the guaranteeing Powers that they should establish a convention at Athens which would periodically regulate Greek instalment payments for the loan. The convention's purpose would be to ease the Greek government's burden of discharging one large annual sum for the interest on the loan as it would give Greece ample time to meet her payments.[178] This was nothing more than a stalling tactic by the administration at Athens and the Powers did not wish to participate. Trikoupis met with the French and Russian representatives in London to discuss the idea of a convention composed of the Powers' representatives at Athens. The Russian ambassador warned that Greece should abandon any demands which it had concerning the use of instalment payments as Public Works funds. Although Gorchakoff supported such demands on the part of Greece in August 1861, the Russian government realized that the Western Powers were against them. The Russian ambassador at London dismissed the Greek government's expectations as extreme and laughable.[179] Lord Russell, however, informed Trikoupis that he would contact St. Petersburg and Paris and present the idea of a convention to those governments for their reaction.

The Cabinet and the Court at Athens realized in the summer of 1861 that they had lost diplomatic support from all three Powers. Since her establishment as a kingdom, Greece managed to neutralize the excesses of each Power in Greece by gaining support of the others. The traditional three party system worked conveniently in Greece for King Otho. During his reign he appointed Francophiles to the cabinet when he opposed British and Russian policies in the Near East. He appointed Russophiles when he opposed the Western Powers and the Ottoman empire and when he wanted to neutralize British diplomacy in Greece and minimize its influence, he appointed politicians from the "Russian" and "French" parties and excluded the Anglophiles. After the Crimean War, however, the gap between the three parties closed and Greek politicians realized that every government wanted to protect its own national interests. Greeks paid less attention to the loyalties of their patron nation and more to their own national interests. Greek national consciousness rapidly developed suspicions about all foreign Powers who interfered in Greek domestic affairs. Otho was partly responsible for closing the gap between the parties for he appointed to the Cabinet and the Senate politicians loyal to him. Many Greeks, however, became disillusioned about their party loyalties after the Franco-British occupation.[180]

The domestic political change in Greece triggered a change of the Powers' policy toward the Protectorate. Russia which had supported Otho since 1850 changed its Greek policy most radically at the end of 1861. The Russian government questioned if its diplomatic support for Greece was worth risking tensions with Great Britain and France. The three Powers had diplomatically confronted each other in Greece because of Otho's change of policies but after the Crimean War there was no reason for them to engage in any confrontations as their Near Eastern interests and policies were counter to those of Greece. In August 1861, Prince Gorchakoff expressed his changing attitude toward Greece. He stated to Napier in St. Petersburg, "I love the Greeks well but I am not insensible to their errors and I do not fail to notice them."[181] At the same time the Russian Foreign Minister expressed his satisfaction with the improved relations between the three Powers' representatives at Athens. He condemned the old system of intrigues and jealousies in the Greek capital and he trusted that they would never recur.[182]

The Russian Foreign Minister agreed with the Western Powers that Greece should upkeep her instalment payments to the guaranteeing governments and not devote those funds for public works.[183] In order to avoid any further confrontations with England and France, Gorchakoff preferred to withdraw his support from Otho's government. Russia opposed Trikoupis's recommendation concerning the establishment of a convention at Athens which regulated the Greek instalment payments. Gorchakoff argued that the Powers had nothing to gain by stipulations of that form and that they should follow the Commission's recommendations in regards to the Greek foreign debt.[184] Lord Russell agreed with Trikoupis on the proposal of the convention because he felt that the convention like the Commission would keep a close watch on Greek finances and secure payments to the Powers.

Gorchakoff, however, still held to the view that any proposal to increase the Greek annual instalments should originate with the Greek Cabinet and not with the guaranteeing governments.[185] He modified his position on this issue which France and England opposed and by the end of August he concurred, without any reservations, with the Commission's conclusions and the Western Powers policy toward Greece. When the Hellenic government requested from the Powers that they deposit and/or spend the instalment funds in Greece, Russia agreed with France and England to deny the Protectorate's request. Finally, Gorchakoff, in his effort to retain cordial relations with the Western Powers, maintained that if the French and British governments insisted on the necessity of a convention at Athens he would ultimately support it.[186]

The three Powers agreed at the end of August to adopt a unanimous course of action towards the Greek foreign debt and its liquidation. Although the guaranteeing governments agreed on their future financial policy toward Greece they did not notify officials at Athens of their decisions. In September the Greek representative at St. Petersburg confidentially learned that London and Paris rejected the Trikoupis proposal for a convention and that Russia concurred with the Western Powers.[187] In Athens the British Legation demanded payment in September for the interest and sinking fund on the loan. Koundouriotes refused to submit any sums to the Legation and maintained that the Powers had not officially notified the King's government about the Trikoupis proposal of a convention. The Foreign Minister had a dismal hope that the Power would approve of the convention. The British Minister at Athens explained the Greek administration's misunderstanding of the Powers' decision concerning the instalment as follows:

> They (Powers) were not unwilling to leave to Greece the initiative in fixing the amount and periods of her future payments, in other words, that it was to be entirely at her choice when and how much she was to pay to her debt, and that we (the Powers) were virtually to surrender the right we now possess under Treaty to interfere, when and how we judged necessary for the execution of existing stipulations.[188]

The Greek government used the "Convention proposal" in order to delay further payments to the Powers. In September 1861 Greece owed 1,800,000 francs to the Powers according to the agreement of 1859 between the Commission and the Administration at Athens. The Greek officials wished to commense payment on the interest and sinking fund in

1862 so they did not include the 1,800,000 francs in the budgets of the two preceeding years.[189] The Powers' Legations at Athens informed the Cabinet that it could not delay payment any longer on the interest and sinking fund charges due in September 1861.[190] Wyse gave the Greek Foreign Ministry a deadline to meet on the instalment payment. Koundouriotes accused Great Britain of resorting to unnecessary financial coersive measures.[191] The British Charge d'Affaires, however, supported by the French and Russian Legations at Athens, demanded from Koundouriotes a complete explanation for the Greek government's neglect of its financial obligations to the Protecting Powers. He also demanded to know why the Ministry did not include the instalment payments in the budgets of 1860 and 1861, and why Greece was willing to pay only one and not both annual instalment payments.[192]

Koundouriotes responded that Greek financial resources could not provide for both annual payments discharged simultaneously as the Powers demanded. The Greek Minister of Finance decided therefore to include only one payment for 1861, that which was due in 1860. Koundouriotes assured the three Powers' representatives that Greece intended to resume regular payments to the guaranteeing governments after 1861.[193] In October 1861, France and Great Britain acknowledged receipt of the Greek instalment payment for the year 1860.[194]

After the British government received the first Greek instalment payment, the Foreign Office issued a statement to the Cabinet at Athens which outlined the official British position on the Powers' agreement of August 1861 concerning their financial policy in Greece.

(1) There is no necessity for any fresh convention to regulate payment of the sums due under the Convention of the 7th May 1832. (2) That Her Majesty's Government cannot consent that the sums due under the said Convention should be applied to the internal improvement of Greece. (3) That the Government of H. H. M. fully accept the Report of the Commission of 1857 with the modification that with respect to any increase on the yearly payments, as suggested by the Commission, the Greek government shall take the initiative.[195]

In conclusion the dispatch which Lord Palmerston designed emphasized that Greece should not delay her payments in the future which were due on the interest and sinking fund. The French and Russian governments fully supported Palmerston's message to Greece and the three Powers pledged not to allow political intrigues in Athens to compromise their solidarity.

During the last year of Otho's reign the Great Powers acted in unison supporting each other's foreign financial policy in Greece. This left Otho without an ally and extremely vulnerable to foreign pressures. The King's government and the Powers experienced a final confrontation before the Greek people sent Otho into exile in 1862. In February 1862, the Administration at Athens negotiated a loan for 2,000,000 drachmas or 1,800,000 francs. The government negotiated the loan with the National Bank of Greece and it proposed to place as security to the Bank a portion of the Custom House duties and certain olive groves in Salona.[196] Like the proposed 5,000,000 drachmas loan of 1853, the loan of 1862 remained a secret from Powers' Legations at Athens. Wyse learned about the proposed loan before the Cabinet officially announced it publicly. He summoned the Russian and French representatives and asked them to join him in submitting a formal protest against the Greek government's proposed loan.[197] The British Charge d'Affaires wrote to the Foreign Office that the Greek loan under negotiation was illegal according to the 1832 Treaty. He also added that when the Greek state attempted to raise the 1853 loan the Powers blocked its efforts effectively because the government in Athens announced its intentions to raise the loan publicly. In 1862, however, negotiations were secret and the officials at Athens did not admit anything about a loan which left the Powers helpless in case they wished to express their protests.

The French and the Russian representatives at Athens followed Eliot's example and informed their governments that the Cabinet secretly negotiated a loan with the National Bank. All three guaranteeing Powers were against the Greek proposed loan.[198] On 25 February 1862, the British bondholders of the 1824 and 1825 loans also protested against the new Greek loan. They argued, as they did in 1853 and on other occasions when Greece wished to mortgage or

distribute her National lands, that the Greek government could not alienate the State property under any circumstances because it was mortgaged for the 1824 and 1825 loans.[199] The French and British governments advised their representatives at Athens to formally protest the
new Greek loan and the alienation of State property.[200]
of State property.[200]

In June the Greek Foreign Minister, under the Powers' pressure, submitted a formal report to the guaranteeing governments' Legations in
which he officially announced that the Administration negotiated a loan
for two million drachmas.[201] The British Minister at Athens immediately
responded to Heliopoulos, the new foreign minister who replaced Koundouriotes, that Great Britain objected to the proposed Greek loan. He
announced his strongest objections against the alienation of the National
lands.

> The novel doctrine of regarding olive groves and such like prop-
> erty in the light of perishable goods of which the Greek govern-
> ment is at liberty to dispose is one which if admitted would
> enable them by degrees to alienate the whole of the National
> Domains and immediately to diminish the revenues of the king-
> dom, the first fruits of which are secured to the Three Powers
> under the Treaty of 1832.[202]

The governments in Paris and St. Petersburg supported Britain's protestations against Greece. Prince Gorchakoff stated to the British ambassador in Russia that Greece had a primary financial responsibility
toward the guaranteeing governments and also toward the British bondholders.[203]

The most important factor about the 1862 loan was that the government negotiated it in order to save the monarchy from the threat of the
revolution which broke out early in 1862. The Greeks revolted against
the monarchy during the first years of Otho's regency in Greece (1834-
36), they revolted in September 1843 and won a Constitution for the
nation, and they revolted again in 1848 without significant results. From
1850 to 1859, Otho diverted the country's attention from domestic
problems to foreign affairs. Anti-Western sentiments in Greece were high
in the 1850s but once the Commission finished its inquiries in 1859 the

people turned their attention to domestic problems. The revolutionary element during Otho's reign was primarily the Greek military, and especially retired officers who resented the monarchy. These were the revolutionaries of the 1830s and 1840s as well as of 1862.

In February and March 1862, an anti-monarchist revolt broke out at Nauplion which ex-military officers directed.[204] In April the government troops contained the revolution at Nauplion but the revolutionary atmosphere spread throughout Greece and could not be prevented.[205] The royalist government and a handful of Greek capitalists who felt the threat of revolution and the uncertain future, negotiated a loan in February for the purpose of defeating the rebels. The Powers knew that the monarchy was threatened by rebellion at Nauplion but they were unwilling to aid Otho just as they did not offer any aid to him during the Constitutional Revolution of 1843.

In June the Greek Foreign Minister, Heliopoulos, attempted to persuade the British Minister at Athens, W. C. Eliot that the government mortgaged only the perishable State property for the new loan. He assured Eliot that the Powers' interests in Greece and those of the bondholders were uneffected by the new loan.[206] Heliopoulos also wrote to Trikoupis in London to inform the Foreign Office that the loan was only for 1,500,000 francs and that the State urgently needed the money after the revolutionary activities in the country. The Greek Foreign Minister assured Great Britain and the other two Powers that Greece mortgaged perishable property only so that no one would raise any objections.[207]

The Powers knew that there was a revolutionary threat to Otho's throne in Greece which would change the political arena in Athens. Thouvenel, the French foreign minister and an old friend of Otho, expressed concern about the revolution and the possibility of Otho's dethronement. The French Foreign Minister believed that the Powers' financial pressure on Otho would certainly accelerate the crisis in Greece. The French Legation at Athens allowed the interest due to France for 1862 to remain in arrear, but demanded from the Hellenic State payment for the 1861 account. The French Charge d'Affaires, his Russian and British colleagues at Athens realized that if Greece was not able to pay the 1862 account it could not afford that of 1861 either. Buree, the French minister at Athens, suggested to Bludoff, the Russian representative in Greece, and to Eliot that the Protecting Powers should be lenient toward Greece which was facing internal uprisings. He maintained, however, that after 1863 the Powers should adopt severe measures to deal with the liquidation of the Greek foreign debt. He stated:

> The Greek government should have due notice that from January 1863 the three Powers should take possession of the Custom Houses and the collection of the money paid at all the Greek ports until the liquidation of the debt.[208]

For the first time during Otho's reign the Powers' representatives agreed that if their governments expected to be paid by Greece they would have to impose financial controls of some type in that nation. This did not occur, however, because Otho was exiled before January 1863.

The governments in London, St. Petersburg and Paris knew the extent of the crisis which Otho faced in 1862. On 28 September they granted the Greek monarch and his government a three month grace period on the instalment payments and then they warned that the guaranteeing Powers would have to impose financial controls in Greece. At a time when the Greek King needed the Powers' support they refused him aid. Otho had alienated the Protecting governments by his own policies. His pro-Russian and anti-Turkish foreign policy antagonized Britain and France. His appointment of royalist Ministries and the growing number of nationalist politicians in Athens alienated the Russians. The Tsar's government after 1860 was less interested in Greek affairs not only because of the closing of the gap between the three parties in Greece, but also because it was more involved in Poland[209] and generally interested in the Slavic Balkan countries rather than Greece. Greece ceased to be the center of attention for a few years in the Near East.

On 11 October 1862, Otho returned to Pireaus from a short trip. Upon his arrival at the port a welcoming committee warned him not to land for he was in danger of loosing his life by the Greek rebels.[210] Otho's exile started and a thirty-year rule by the Bavarian dynasty ended. With it ended an era of government corruption, oppression and intrigue by the Greek court. Otho's accomplishments in Greece were all negative. He did nothing for the nation's economy, the Public Treasury suffered enormous deficits during his reign, and the Greek foreign debt increased considerably as he was unconcerned to dissolve it. The following chart outline the arrears due to Great Britain from 1844 to 1863.

Issued out of the Consolidated
Fund, in the undermentioned
years, for payment of thee
Interest and Sinking Fund
on that portion of the Greek
Loan which had been guaranteed

by this Country:—vis.,	£	s.	d.[211]
in 1843 33,583		17	1
in 1844 46,784		4	8
in 1845 46,497		4	—
in 1846 46,497		4	—
in 1847 47,188		9	7
in 1848 46,749		13	1
in 1849 47,049		5	8
in 1850 46,955		18	8
in 1851 47,541		8	8
in 1852 47,118		9	10
in 1853 47,637		1	2
in 1854 47,637		1	2
in 1855 47,494		8	1
in 1856 47,048		11	11
in 1857 47,258		16	—
in 1858 47,471		2	11
in 1859 47,494		8	1
in 1860 47,518		2	10
in 1861 47,048		14	8
in 1862 47,423		9	6
in 1863 47,282		6	11
	977,279	18	6

Repaid by the Greek	£	s.	d.
Government			
in 1847 23,343		16	2
in 1848 7,740		15	6
in 1861 3,944		14	4
	35,029	6	—
Balance due by the Greek			
Goverment	942,250	12	6

The total amount shown above which Greece owed to Great Britain was one third of the total she owed for the loan of 1832 on the interest and sinking fund.

Otho's inability to deal effectively in his financial relations with the Powers resulted in continuous foreign interference into Greek internal affairs. In 1850 Great Britain blockaded Greece partly because of financial disputes between the two nations. From 1854 to 1857 Greece suffered a Franco-British occupation because Otho was more interested in using the public funds to fight the Turks than he was in using them to dissolve the country's foreign debt. From 1857 to 1859 the Financial Commission was established because Otho and his puppet ministries refused to meet their financial obligations toward the Powers. Finally, the Greek people drove Otho from power. The Powers who forced him upon Greece in 1832 helped to dethrone him by imposing financial pressures on Greece during the last years of his reign.

The Bavarian dynasty ended an era of tyrannical and irresponsible rule, but it did not end the European interference in Greek domestic affairs. In the last analysis the Powers were just as guilty as Otho for the thirty year period of misrule, corruption, intrigue and oppression in Greece. The continuous struggle between the three Powers to exercise a dominant role in the Greek government throughout Otho's reign had the most devasting consequences for the Greek people. From patronizing Greek politicians, to occupying the country, to installing a financial commission, the Powers violated the 1832 Treaty which guaranteed the independence and sovereignty of the Greek State.

CONCLUSION

Greek foreign borrowing from 1824 to 1836 was beneficial to resurgent Greece in limited respects. The provisional government of 1824 and 1825 resorted to foreign loans for various reasons. (A) It needed to consolidate its power and unify the revolution around the Hydriot based government. (B) It needed European financial, moral and diplomatic support to continue its struggle against the Ottoman empire. And (C) the loans provided financial strength and recognition of legitimacy for the revolutionary government by the European community. These were the reasons for the necessity of foreign borrowing by the provisional government.

The price which the government paid, however, for these loans during Otho's reign was British interference in Greek domestic affairs. Greece defaulted her payments to the British bondholders and the Foreign Office used that as a legitimate excuse to prevent the government in Athens from exercising its sovereignty over the State property. This partial financial control in Greece by England would not have taken place if the provisional government had not contracted the large loans in 1824 and 1825 which had little positive value for the Revolution. The first loans therefore provided few benefits for the Revolution but they burdened the nation throughout the nineteenth century and gave Great Britain a legitimate excuse to intervene in Greek internal affairs.

The guaranteed loan of 1832 was also necessary from the sovereign's point of view. The nation had an empty Treasury, there was a need to establish a government bureaucracy and the King of Greece had to be provided with military protection. Like the first two loans, therefore, the 1832 loan provided a service for the government but it did not provide any services for the governed. Apart from the creation of a government bureaucracy designed to keep Otho in power, the guaranteed loan did not yield any benefits to Greece.

Like the first two loans, that of 1832 inflicted more damages to the country than it brought benefits. First, it was not submitted all at once in 1833 and the government's expenditure forced Otho to contract another short term loan from Bavaria. So Greece kept increasing her foreign debt but the nation's resources did not increase as rapidly in order to meet the payments on all the foreign loans. The country defaulted and the result of her default was blatant interference by the Powers in Greek domestic affairs.

King Otho's governments did not introduce progressive economic and financial reforms and they were not able to liquidate the nation's foreign debt during his reign. The regenerated Greek nation showed few signs of significant economic changes and progress during her first thirty years of independence. Greek financial relations with the Powers during Otho's reign were therefore strained by the government's inability to revitalize the country's economic resources and meet its foreign financial obligations. During the last decade of Otho's reign the Western Powers pursued a policy of interventionism in Greece and exercised partial financial control in the Protectorate. Article XII of the Treaty of 1832 gave the Powers the right to intervene in Greece and to exercise their prerogative of financial control in that country. Because of the guaranteed loan and of Otho's inability to dissolve the nation's foreign debt the Greek people endured the calamities which the Powers inflicted upon them throughout the nineteenth century.

In 1862 King Otho paid the price of exile for his incompetent ruling of Greece. The Powers, however, did not allow the Greeks to determine their own political fate and as in 1832 they chose a king to rule their Protectorate. On 30 March 1863, France, Great Britain and Russia selected Prince William George of Denmark to become King of the Hellenes. They justified their intervention in Greece's political future as follows:

> . . . events which had recently taken place in Greece (the Revolution of 1862) could not effect the firm resolution of the three Courts by common consent to *watch over* the maintenance of the repose, of the independence, and of the prosperity of the

Hellenic Kingdom which France, Great Britain and Russia contributed to found, in the general interest of civilization, or order, and of peace.[1]

The Powers justified their continuing policy of interventionism in the nineteenth century in the name of civilization, order, prosperity and peace for Greece.

APPENDIX A

THE ABBOTT CASE

During Otho's reign Great Britain had economic interests in Greece which the British Legation at Athens protected. There were many cases which involved grievances between the Greek government and British subjects' interests in Greece in which the Foreign Office intervened. The British blockade in 1850 and the Currant traders grievances in the 1850s were clear cases of blatant British intervention in Greek internal affairs.[1] Another case of unjustified British intervention in Greece involved Richard B. Abbott an English entrepreneur.

On 10 October 1852 Abbott started work for a British company that contracted the Naxos emery mines from the Greek government. His contract was for ten years, and he was responsible for discharging 110,100 drachmas quarterly to the Greek government for exploiting the emery mines at Naxos. According to his contract Abbott was responsible for the quarterly payments to the State whether he cleared any profits or not from the mines.[2] He deposited 75,000 drachmas downpayment to the Public Treasury as security and in 1852 and 1853 he made the agreed quarterly payments to the State Treasury. In 1854, however, he only made the first two payments and thereafter paid nothing to the Public Treasury.[3]

Abbott and his attorney, G. Villios argued that the Greek Treasury owed him money and that he did not owe anything to the government. He sued the Ministry of Finance and held it liable for damages which he suffered as result of its harassment. The government revoked the Abbott contract on 23 December 1856[4] after he failed to make any payments since September 1854. After the contract was revoked, the Administration contacted the British and French representatives at Athens to inform them that the Naxos emery mines were open for bidding.

The Greek government invited Abbott to resolve his difference with the Ministry of Finance in the Greek Courts. Abbott, however, did not believe that his case would have been justly resolved in the courts so he resorted to the British Legation. In April 1857, Wyse contacted Ragabes and demanded to have explicit details on the Greek government's action against Abbott.[5] The Ministry of Finance prepared a laborious report which outlined the entire history of the Abbott case. According to the report Abbott violated the terms of his contract, and although the State gave him ample time to meet his payments to the Treasury he failed to carry out his financial obligations toward Greece.[6]

Wyse's reaction to the report was extremely negative. He accused the State of illegally revoking the Abbott contract and depriving him of his legitimate right to the Naxos mines. The British Minister refused to accept the government's word that Abbott violated the terms of his contract and he charged that Abbott could not find justice in Greek courts which were controlled by the Administration. Finally, Wyse informed Ragabes that Abbott lost his employment from the British company with which he was associated because the Greek government ruptured his contract in December 1856.[7] "This course," the British Charge d'Affaires wrote, "will naturally expose him to losses for which the government will become, as happening through their act, responsible . . . ."[8] The reasons that Wyse was eager to protect Abbott's interest were due to many factors, some political and others economic.

When the Administration announced that the Naxos emery mines were open for bidding, the French Charge d'Affaires, Mercier, wrote to Ragabes that a French company had an interest in the mines.[9] Mercier, however, wanted to make certain that there were no legal complications involved with Abbott before any one else took over the mines. The Greek government was eager to have French rather than British entrepreneurs exploit the Naxos mines. Throughout the Franco-British occupation of Greece, Otho's diplomatic efforts aimed at British diplomatic isolation in Greece by displaying the Cabinet's and Court's favoritism toward the French. In March the government at Athens asked Walewski to provide Greece with French technical advisors and especially mining engineers to advise the Greek officials.[10] Greek favoritism toward France had a negative impact at the British Legation in Athens and it accounted for Wyse's anger toward the Administration.

When Wyse's dispatch about the Abbott case reached the Ministry of Finance, the officials in that Department were furious with his insults to the Greek government. Wyse insulted the Departments of Justice and Finance as well as the entire Cabinet. The Minister of Finance responded first by questioning British justice just as Wyse questioned Greek justice. Then he explained that the Greek government did not force Abbott to sign the contract for the Naxos mines, and the Cabinet certainly had nothing to do with his failure to meet his payments to the Treasury. The Ministry insisted that the Abbott case was clearly a matter for the Greek courts to solve and it should not have involved other parties in it. Finally, the Greek Minister of Finance, emphasized that his government resented British diplomatic interference in Greek domestic affairs.[11]

The government demanded 525,000 drachmas in arrears from Abbott but he did not remit any sum to the Treasury. The Greek court ruled against him and his contract remained revoked.[12] The Ministry of Finance was indeed correct to rupture the Abbott contract because he did not, contrary to his claim, pay the quarterly dues after the second quarter of 1854. On 18 July 1858, the Ministry of Finance submitted a thart to the Financial Commission which outlined the dates and amounts which Abbott paid to the Treasury for use of the Naxos mines.

Year	Receipts[13]
1852	440,400
1853	440,400
1854	220,200
1855	—
1856	—

The Abbott case was just another among many in which Great Britain's diplomatic services were used to protect British economic interests in Greece. Unlike other cases, however, such as the Pacifico and Finlay,[14] the will of the British Legation did not prevail in the Abbott case only because the French economic interests countered it. The blatant British interference in Greek domestic affairs was a frequent phenomenon during Otho's reign and it exemplified Great Britain's antagonisms with Greece and with the other Protecting Powers.

Grain Trade[17]

Year	Imports (Value)	Exports (Value)	Difference (Value)
1851	5,048,088 dr.	365,963 dr.	4,682,125 dr.
1852	7,822,295	389.066	7,433,229
1853	2,759,394	548,528	2,210,866
1854	5,621,839	155,732	5,466,107
1855	7,310,007	—	—
1856	9,866,097	747,088	9,119,009
1857	3,800,527	655,835	3,144,692
1858	3,752,912	1,092,508	2,660,404
1859	7,226,731	527,522	6,699,209
1860	9,730,636	202,971	9,527,665
1861	6,345,987	471,893	5,874,094
1862	3,822,192	393,367	3,428,825

APPENDIX B

Population Statistics During Otho's Reign[15]

Year	Population	Population Increase	Residents per Square Kilometer
1821	938,765	—	19.17
1828	753,400	− 185,365	15.86
1838	752,077	—	15.83
1839	823,773	+ 71,696	17.34
1840	850,246	+ 26,473	17.89
1841	861,019	+ 10,773	18.12
1842	853,005	− 8,014	17.95
1843	915,059	+ 67,054	19.26
1844	930,295	+ 15,236	19.58
1845	960,236	+ 29,941	20.21
1848	986,731	+ 26,495	20.77
1853	1,042,527	+ 55,795	—
1856	1,062,627	+ 20,100	—
1861	1,096,810	+ 34,183	—

Land Statistics During Otho's Reign[16]

Land Type	Stremmata
Cultivated	7,435,900
Tillable uncultivated	11,748,000
Mountains and Pastures	18,599,240
Forests	5,419,660
Swamps	833,448
Cities, Villages, Roads, Rivers, etc.	1,653,000

NOTES

Notes to Chapter 1

1. For different views on the organization and accomplishments of the *Philiki Etairia* see Douglas Dakin, *The Greek Struggle for Independence, 1821-1833* (Berkley, 1973), 41-60, Richard Clogg, ed., *The Struggle for Greek Independence* (London, 1973), 87-100, 200-19, Epameinodas K. Kyriakides, *Istoria tou Synchronou Ellenismou apo tes Edryseos tou Vasileiou tes Ellados, 1832-1892* (History of Contemporary Greeks from the Founding of the Kingdom of Greece, 1832-1892) (Athens, 1972), I, 52-65, Tasos Vournas, *Istoria tes Neoteres Elladas* (History of Modern Greece) (Athens, 1974), 63-74, and B. Mexas, *Oi Philikoi* (Athens, 1973), which is a detailed account of the Etairia and its main characters.

2. For details on the factions' struggles for power during the first years of the Revolution see George Finlay, *History of the Greek Revolution and the Reign of King Otho* (London, 1971), I, 133-35, 234-47, John Anthony Petropoulos, *Politics and Statecraft in the Kingdom of Greece, 1833-1843* (Princeton, 1968), 76-87.

3. Finlay, *History,* I, 227.

4. The local leaders of the Revolution were divided into two categories; the Primates or Kodja Bashis and the chieftains, or Armatoloi and Kleftes (Armed Policemen and Brigandes). The Primates were the tyranical Greek upper class of the mainland. They served in local Turkish administration at the Greek populated provinces as Tax Collectors. The Chieftains were popular among the Greeks of the mainland for they fought against the Kodja Bashis who exploited the agrarian population of the Provinces. For more details see Richard Clogg, ed., *The Movement for Greek Independence, 1770-1821* (London, 1976), 21-22, Finlay, *History,* I, 11, 19-26, Petropoulos, *Kingdom of Greece,* 27-34, and for an in-depth look at the chieftains see Tasos Vournas, *Armatoloi kai Kleftes* (Athens, 1958).

5. A.M. Andreades, *Erga* (Works (Athens, 1938-1940), II, 303.

6. Vournas, *History,* 111.

7. Andreades, *Works,* II, 313.

8. According to Andreades, *Works,* II, 303-05, 1,000,000 grosia was collected in 1823 from contributions in Greece. European Philhellenes sent to the struggling nation 174,000 dollars, and Lord Byron who was largely responsible for publicising the Greek cause of Independence, loaned 4,000 pounds sterling to Greece. This sum was remitted to Byron in 1824 when the Greeks contracted their first foreign loan.

9. N.P. Diamandouros, ed., *Hellenism and the First War of Liberation, 1821-1830,* Thessalonike, 1976), 119.

10. Tasos Lignades, *E Xenike Exartises kata ten Diadromen tou Neoellinikou Kratous, 1821-1945* (The Foreign Dependence During the Course of the Modern Greek State, 1821-1945) (Athens, 1975), 61, also see Diamandouros, *War of Liberation,* 113-14.

11. Vournas, *History,* 111.

12. For the most complete biography of John Kapodistrias see C.M. Woodhouse, *Capodistrias: The Founder of Greek Independence* (London, 1973, also see William P. Kaldis, *John Kapodistrias and the Modern Greek State* (Madison, 1963).

13. Under the Turkish system 1 stremma equalled 0.314 acre; the Greek Royal stremma equalled to 0.247 acre. Diamandouros, *War of Liberation,* 114. For the Kapodistrian report on the status of the National and private property see A. Sideris, *E. Georgike Politike tes Ellados kata ten Lexasan Ekatontaetian* (The Agricultural Policy of Greece During the Last One Hundred Years) (Athens, 1933), 26.

14. Giannes Kordatos, *Istoria tes Neoteres Elladas* (History of Modern Greece) (Athens, 1957-58), II, 454, also see Andreades, *Works,* II, 301.

15. Kordatos, *Modern Greece,* II, 455.

16. Andreades, *Works,* II, 300-01.

17. Diamandouros, *War of Liberation,* 120.

18. Andreades, *Works,* II, 303.

19. Vournas, *History,* 125-27, Diamandouros, *War of Liberation,* 120-22. For the most detailed account on Greek agriculture and the National Estates controversy during the Revolution see Demetrios L. Zographos, *Istoria Ellenikes Georgias, 1821-1833* (History of Greek Agriculture, 1821-1833) (Athens, 1923), I, covers the period from the outbreak of the Revolution to the election of Kapodistrias.

20. Lignades, *Greek State,* 67.

21. There are numerous works on European diplomatic opposition to the Greek War of Independence. For Metternichian opposition to the struggle see Henry Kissinger, *A World Restored* (Boston, 1973), 290-96. For a general outlook of the issue see M.S. Anderson, *The Eastern Question, 1774-1923* (New York, 1968), 58-61, and J.A.R. Marriott, *The Eastern Question* (Oxford, 1969), 194-97.

22. For details on the European Philhellenes before 1821 see C.M. Woodhouse, *The Philhellenes* (Madison, 1971), 13-39.

23. Anastasios Lignades, *To Proton Daneion tes Anexartesias* (The First Loan of Independence) (Athens, 1970), 24.

24. John A. Levandis, *The Greek Foreign Debt and the Great Powers, 1821-1898* (New York, 1944), 6.

25. Lignades, *The First Loan,* 93-97.

26. Leland H. Jenks, *The Migration of British Capital to 1875* (New York, 1927), 45.

27. David Howarth, *The Greek Adventure* (New York, 1976), 119.

28. Dakin, *Greek Independence,* 109.

29. Woodhouse, *Philhellenes,* 66-93.

30. For complete details on the London Greek Committee see Lignades, *The First Loan,* 45-61.

31. For a profile on Alexander Mavrokordatos' early life and career see, Andreas S. Skandames, *Selides Politikes Istorias kai Kritikes, E. Triakontaetia tes Vasileias tou Othonos, 1832-1862* (Pages of Political History and Critique, the Thirty-Year Kingdom of Otho, 1832-1862) (Athens, 1961), 604-19.

32. Lignades, *The First Loan,* 63-64.

33. Petropoulos, *Kingdom of Greece,* 70-71, 76-82.

34. For details on the career and political affiliations of the legendary Kolokotrones see Theodore Kolokotrones, *Memoires from the Greek War of Independence, 1821-1833,* trans. by G. Tertzetis (Chicago, 1969).

35. Dakin, *Greek Independence,* 109.

36. Levandis, *Greek Foreign Debt,* 6-8, also see William St. Clair, *That Greece Might Still Be Free* (London, 1972), 129-30.

37. Lignades, *The First Loan,* 97-8.

38. *Ibid.,* 99-100.

39. Cited in Woodhouse, *Philhellenes,* 79.

40. For more on Greek commercial progress from 1770 to 1821 see Clogg, ed., *The Movement for Greek Independence,* 22-45, also see D.A. Zakynthinos, *The Making of Modern Greece,* trans. by K.R. Johnston (Oxford, 1976), 131-39, and Giannes Kordatos, *E Koinonike Semasia tes Ellenikes Epanastaseos tou 1821* (The Social Significance of the Greek Revolution of 1821) (Athens, 1946), 56-71.

41. Woodhouse, *Philhellenes,* 78-80.

42. Lignades, *The First Loan,* 159-60.

43. Levandis, *Greek Foreign Debt,* 8-11.

44. Kordatos, *Modern Greece,* II, 455.

45. *Koundouriotou Archeia,* ed. A. Lignos (Pireaus, 1920-1927), II,81.

46. Lignades, *The First Loan,* 163-64.

47. *Ibid.,* 166.

48. *Ibid.,* 167.

49. *Koundouriotou Archeia,* II, 129.

50. *Ibid.,* II, 130.

51. Lignades, *The First Loan,* 168-69.

52. *Ibid.,* 168-69.

53. *Koundouriotou Archeia,* II, 130.

54. Howarth, *Greek Adventure,* 170.

55. Lignades, *The First Loan,* 174.

56. Levandis, *Greek Foreign Debt,* 14-15, and Lignades, *The First Loan,* 172.

57. Phanar was the Greek district in Constantinople from which many prominent Greeks such as A. Mavrokordatos came to join the Revolution.

58. Levandis, *Greek Foreign Debt,* 15.

59. Jenks, *British Capital,* 44-9.

60. Kordatos, *Modern Greece,* II, 455.

61. Among the most important are, Lignades, *The First Loan,* 182, Levandis, *Greek Foreign Debt,* 15, and D. Kokkinos, *E Ellenike Epanastasis* (The Greek Revolution) (Athens, 1931-1935), I, 245.

62. Levandis, *Greek Foreign Debt,* 15.

63. For the early career of John Kolettes see Skandames, *Kingdom of Otho,* 638-47.

64. George Jarvis, *His Journal and Related Documents,* ed. G.D. Arnakis (Thessalonike, 1965), 181.

65. *Ibid.*, 181.

66. Andreades, *Works,* II, 306-09.

67. The first funds arrived in Zante from London on 12/24 April 1824 on the ship "Florida." The sum was £44,000, and it was given to Barf Banking House and the Logothetis Bank. Lignades, *The First Loan,* 253.

68. Many Greek shipowners of the Islands like the Koundouriotes family were Greek-Albanians and they played a decisive role during the Revolution. For details on the Albanians during the Revolution see Finlay, *History,* I, 28-52.

69. *Ibid.,* I, 337-38.

70. Petropoulos, *Kingdom of Greece,* 85-89.

71. Finlay, *History,* I, 338.

72. Lignades, *The First Loan,* 393-98.

73. Andreades, *Works,* II, 301, also Vournas, *History,* 111, and Kokkinos, *Greek Revolution,* I, 219.

74. Finlay, *History,* I, 340.

75. At Hydra the Koundouriotes family wealth was esteemed at 2,141,896 grosia, the Vouvaris wealth at 764,114, and the Tompazes at 559,170 grosia. At Spetzas the wealth of Anargyros was valued at 609,000 grosia, of Botasses 453,000, and of Mexes 430,000. At Psara, the wealth of Kotzia was esteemed at 459,000 grosia, and that of Apostolou 448,133. These were the wealthiest of the Greek families most of whose origin was Albanian. Andreades, *Works,* II, 305.

76. Finlay, *History,* I, 338.

77. Levandis, *Greek Foreign Debt,* 16.

78. Kowarth, *Greek Adventure,* 198.

79. *Koundouriotou Archives,* IV, 96-100.

80. Vournas, *History,* 147.

81. *Koundouriotou Archives,* IV, 58-59.

82. Lignades, *Greek State,* 96.

83. Kordatos, *Modern Greece,* II, 456.

84. *Ibid.,* II, 456-57.

85. Lignades, *The First Loan,* 172.

86. Lignades, *Greek State,* 98.

87. Woodhouse, *Philhellenes,* 132.

88. S.B. Markezines, *Politike Istoria tes Neoteras Ellados* (Political History of Modern Greece) (Athens, 1966), I, 30-31.

89. Vournas, *History,* 147.

90.　Levandis, *Greek Foreign Debt,* 24.

91.　*The Greek Loans of 1824 and 1825,* ed. P.S. King (London, 1873), 15.

92.　According to Woodhouse, *Philhellenes,* 132, the British ship-building company delivered all the steamships to Greece but they arrived after the Battle of Navarino thus they did not make any contribution to the War. Vournas, *History,* 148, claimed that only one ship arrived in Greece. Jenks, *British Capital,* 51, claimed that Cochrarie arrived in 1828 with two small ships, Markezines, *History,* I 29, maintained that the British sent "Karteria" only to Greece and no other vessel. What is certain is that the Greeks overpaid for ships which did not aid their struggle.

93.　Ibrahim Pasha was the son of Mohamed Ali, Pasha of Egypt (1805-1849). Ibrahim was commander of the Egyptian fleet which fought at the infamous Battle of Navarino in October 1827. For details see Dakin, *Greek Independence,* 220-30, and Finlay, *History,* I, 343-97.

94.　*The Greek Loan of 1824 and 1825,* 15.

95.　Lignades, *Greek State,* 98.

96.　Cited in *The Greek Loans of 1824-1825,* 44-45.

97.　Cited in Kordatos, *Modern Greece,* II, 459-60.

98.　For details on Kapodistrias' career as a Russian diplomat see Woodhouse, *Capodistrias,* 34-126, also Kaldis, *Kapodistrias,* 3-17.

99.　Sideris, *Agricultural Policy,* 26.

100.　The first civil war lasted from November 1823 to June 1824 with intervals of peace. The second lasted from November to December 1824 and the third from July to August 1827 just a few months before Kapodistrias' arrival in Greece. For details on the civil wars see Petropoulos, *Kingdom of Greece,* 85-88, and Dakin, *Greek Independence,* 218-20.

101.　Finlay, *History,* I, 437.

102.　For a thorough examination of Greek economic development from the Treaty of Kutchuk-Kainardji in 1774 to the outbreak of the Revolution see Kostes Moskof, *E Ethnike kai Koinonike Syneidese sten Ellada, 1830-1909* (The National and Social Conscience in Greece, 1830-1909) (Athens, 1974), 83-91, also see Vournas, *History,* 20-23. On the decay of Greek economic life during the Revolution see Sideris, *Agricultural Policy,* 24-26.

103.　Moskof, *Conscience in Greece,* 103.

104. Woodhouse, *Capodistrias,* 403-04. For a detailed account on Kapodistrias' plans for agrarian reforms in Greece see Zographos, *History,* 7-69.

105. Cited in Kaldis, *Kapodistrias,* 97.

106. Lignades, *Greek State,* 77.

107. G. Anastasopoulos, *Istoria tes Ellenikes Viomechanias, 1840-1940* (History of Greek Industry, 1840-1940) (Athens, 1947), I, 101.

108. Kordatos, *Modern Greece,* II, 665.

109. Chrysos Evelpides, *E Georgia tes Ellados* (Greek Agriculture) (Athens, 1944), 44, also see Lignades, *Greek State,* 71.

110. Moskof, *Conscience in Greece,* 139.

111. George Aspreas, *Politike Istoria tes Neoteras Ellados* (Political History of Modern Greece) (Athens, no date), I, 72.

112. Andreades, *Works,* II, 318.

113. Kyriakides, *History,* I, 144, also see Anderson, *Eastern Question,* 75, and Kaldis, *Kapodistrias,* 97-99.

114. Kaldis, *Kapodistrias,* 99.

115. For details on Kapodistrias' policies see Petropoulos, *Kingdom of Greece,* 107-19.

116. Kapodistrias visited London in August 1827 and Paris in October the same year. He was not welcomed by the Foreign Office and was snobbed by Charles X. Kaldis, *Kapodistrias,* 97-100.

117. C.W. Crawley, *The Question of Greek Independence* (Cambridge, 1930), 101.

118. *Ibid.,* 102-03.

119. Andreades, *Works,* II, 322, also see Dakin, *Greek Independence,* 246-47.

120. For details on the assassination of Kapodistrias see Demetris Fotiades, *Othonas: E Monarchia* (Otho: The Monarchy) (Athens, 1963), 53-55.

121. Andreades, *Works,* II, 318.

122. Woodhouse, *Capodistrias,* 405.

123. Andreades, *Works,* II, 324.

124. Finlay, *History,* II, 46.

125. G. Charitakes, *E Ellenike Viomechania* The Greek Industry) (Athens, 1927), 9.

126. Vournas, *History,* 219. The most detailed study on Greek agriculture during the Kapodistrian period is Zographos, *Greek Agriculture,* II.

127. Lignades, *Greek State,* 74.

128. Vournas, *History,* 218-19.

Notes to Chapter 2

1. British and Foreign State Papers, 1826-1827, XIV, 632-38.

2. L.Th. Laskaris, *Diplomatike Istoria tes Ellados, 1821-1914* (Diplomatic History of Greece, 1821-1914) (Athens, 1947), 40-42, also see Dakin, *Greek Independence,* 270.

3. F.O. 32/487, *Confidential,* Memorandum, Foreign Office, January 6, 1871.

4. K. Strupp, ed., *La Situation International de la Gréce, 1821-1917; Recueil de documents choisis et édités avec une introduction historique et dogmatique* (Zurich, 1918), 101-05.

5. Levandis, *Greek Foreign Debt,* 33.

6. F.O. 32/487, *Confidential,* Memorandum, Foreign Office, January 6, 1871.

7. Dakin, *Greek Independence,* 278.

8. Aspreas, *Modern Greece,* I, 110, and Levandis, *Greek Foreign Debt,* 34.

9. F.O. 32/487, *Confidential,* Memorandum, Foreign Office, January 6, 1871.

10. Dakin, *Greek Independence,* 279.

11. F.O. 32/487, *Confidential,* Memorandum, Foreign Office, January 6, 1871.

12. Kyriakides, *History,* I, 213-14, and Aspreas, *Modern Greece,* I, 111.

13. F.O. 32/487, *Confidential,* Memorandum, Foreign Office, January 6, 1871.

14. For details on Otho's early life and his family background see Fotiades, *The Monarchy,* 63-74.

15. Laskaris, *Diplomatic History,* 46.

16. For the full text of the Treaty in Greek see Kyriakides, *History,* I, 216-19.

17. F.O. 32/487, *Confidential,* Memorandum, Foreign Office, January 6, 1871.

18. *Ibid.*

19. Andreades, *Works,* II, 333, and Levandis, *Greek Foreign Debt,* 37.

20. Levandis, *Greek Foreign Debt,* 39-40.

21. A.Y.E. 1856, 8/1, (unnumbered) Exposé général de la gestion de l'emprunt Rothchild de francs 60 millions, Athénes, (no date).

22. Andreades, *Works,* II, 334.

23. Casimir Laconte, *Etude Economique de la Gréce* (Paris, 1847), 155.

24. Petropoulos, *Kingdom of Greece,* 169.

25. Fotiades, *The Monarchy,* 155.

26. *Ibid.,* 90.

27. British and Foreign State Papers, 1834-1835, XXIII, 959-60.

28. F.O. 32/487 (unnumbered) *Confidential,* Memorandum, Foreign Office, December 1874.

28a. For an account of Palmerston's early career as Foreign Secretary see C.F. Webster, *The Foreign Policy of Palmerston, 1830-1841* (London, 1951), 2 vols.

29. British and Foreign State Papers, 1834-1835, XXiii, 968.

30. *Ibid.,* XXIII, 961-65, 972-77.

31. Finlay, *History,* II, 156-57.

32. British and Foreign State Papers, 1836-1837, XXIV, 745. For details on the revolts of 1834-1836 see Petropoulos, *Kingdom of Greece,* 218-25, 252-53.

33. Levandis, *Greek Foreign Debt,* 42.

34. Russia was dissatisfied with Armansperg because he favored the two Western Powers and had alienated the Russian influence in Greece. For complete details on this issue see Barbara Jelavich, *Russia and Greece During the Regency of King Otho, 1832-1835* (Thessalonike, 1962), 30-32.

35. The authoritative account concerning the origin and development of the Greek political parties in the nineteenth century is Petropoulos, *Kingdom of Greece,* 4-13, 134-44. Also see Aspreas, *Modern Greece,* I, 28-32.

36. For a complete text of the Constitution see Alexander Svolos, *Ta Ellenika Syntagmata, 1822-1952* (The Greek Constitutions, 1822-1952) (Athens, 1972), 93-110. For an analysis of the first Constitution during Otho's reign see *Ibid.* , 32-33, also see G.D. Daskalakes, *Ellenike Syntagmatike Istoria, 1821-1935* (Greek Constitutional History, 1821-1935) (Athens, 1951), 47-55.

37.   A.Y.E. 1844, 8/1, (unnumbered) An Account of the Distribution of the A and B Series of the Loan, Athens.

38.   British and Foreign State Papers, 1836-1837, XXIV, 748-49.

39.   *Ibid.*, XXIV, 746-47.

40.   *Ibid.* XXIV, 756-61.

41.   *Ibid.*, XXIV, 763-67.

42.   Hansard's Debates, 3rd series, XXXV, 615-38.

43.   F.O. 32/487, *Confidential*, Memorandum, Foreign Office, December 1874, also see British and Foreign State Papers, 1836-1837, XXIV, 497-98.

44.   A.Y.E. 1835, 8/2, (unnumbered) Mavrokordatos to Otho, Munich, June 29/July 11, 1835.

45.   A.Y.E. 1935, 8/2, No. 3209, Othon, Athens, September 23, 1835.

46.   A.Y.E. 1835, 8/2, (unnumbered) Alexander Mavrokordatos, Munich, June 30/July 12, 1835.

47.   Vournas, *History*, 266. According to the Greek budget of 1837, Bavaria advanced 2,229,086 drachmas to Greece. See British and Foreign State Papers, 1837-1838, XXVI, 126.

48.   Petropoulos, *Kingdom of Greece*, 243-45.

49.   For details on the King's marriage to Amalia see Fotiades, *The Monarchy*, 169-83.

50.   For more on the Armansperb dismissal see Kyriakides, *History*, I, 316-17, also Petropoulos, *Kingdom of Greece*, 268-69.

51.   Fotiades, *The Monarchy*, 184-88, see also Aspreas, *Modern Greece*, I, 150-54, and Kyriakides, *History*, I, 323-24.

52.   Aspreas, *Modern Greece*, I, 155-56.

53.   Kyriakides, *History*, I, 323-24.

54.   L. Bower and G. Bolitho, *Otho I: King of Greece, a Biography* (London, 1939), 101-06.

55.   Fotiades, *The Monarchy*, 208, and Kyriakides, *History*, I, 334-36.

56.   F.O. 32/487, *Confidential*, Memorandum, Foreign Office, November 23, 1874.

57.   Petropoulos, *Kingdom of Greece*, 299-305.

58.   *Ibid.*, 317-18.

59.   Kyriakides, *History*, I, 348-49.

60.   Levandis, *Greek Foreign Debt*, 44-45.

61.   F.O. 32/487, *Confidential*, Memorandum, Foreign Office, November 23, 1874.

62.   For details on the Constitutional Revolution of 1843 see Giannes Makrygiannes, *Makrygianne Apomnemoneumata* (Makrygianne Memoirs) (Athens, 1972), 264-75, also see Petropoulos, *Kingdom of Greece*, 442-52, and Fotiades, *The Monarchy*, 281-340.

63.   The only support which Otho had in 1843 was his father's moral support. For details on the Powers' role in the 1843 Revolution in Athens see Barbara Jelavich, *Russia and the Greek Revolution of 1843* (Munich, 1966), 24-45.

64.   For an analysis of the 1843 Constitution and the period of Constitutional Monarchy (1843-62) see Daskalakes, *Constitutional History*, 55-64, also see Svolos, *Constitutions*, 34-37. For the complete text of the 1843 Constitution see *Ibid.*, 111-26.

65.   Hansard's Debates, 3rd series, LXIX, 1096-98.

66.   *Ibid.*, XCII, 24.

67.   *Ibid.*, LXIX, 1096-98. The notes which the three Powers' representatives sent to the Hellenic government are cited in Jelavich, *Greek Revolution*, 49-52.

68.   *Ibid.*, 51.

69.   Hansard's Debates, 3rd series, LXXI, 807.

70.   *Ibid.*, LXXI, 807.

71.   For details on the political instability which followed the 1843 Revolution until August 1844 see Nikolaos Dragoumes, *Istorikai Anamneseis* (Historical Recollections) (Athens, 1925), 3rd ed., II, 74-118, also see Fotiades, *The Monarchy*, 281-340. For more on Kolettes' appointment to office see Dragoumes, *Recollections*, II, 122-27 and Kyriakides, *History*, I, 522-24.

72.   For a complete profile of John Kolettes see Skandames, *Kingdom of Otho*, 638-78, see also Aspreas, *Modern Greece*, I, 192-210, and Demitris Fotiades, *Othonas: E Exosis* (Otho: The Exile) (Athens, 1975), 29-72.

73.   For more on Kolettes' foreign policy see Jon V. Kofas, *International and Domestic Politics in Greece During the Crimean War* (New York, 1980), 9-14.

74.   According to Douglas Johnson, *Guizot: Aspects of French History, 1787-1874* (Toronto, 1963), 275, 309-12, Francois Guizot placed his confidence blindly in Kolettes and he supported the Greek Prime Minister during his three years in office.

75.   For a general outlook of Anglo-French relations from 1841 to 1854 see G. D. Clayton, *Britain and the Eastern Question: Messolonghi to Gallipoli* (London, 1871), 94-103, also see Anderson, *Eastern Question,* 116-138.

76.   A. Y. E. 1844, 8/1, No. 6, Lord Aberdeen to Greek Minister of Foreign Affairs, Athens, February 16/28, 1844.

77.   A. Y. E. 1844, 8/1, No. 334, Lyons to Greek Minister of Foreign Affairs, Athens, February 12, 1844.

78.   A. Y. E. 1844, 8/1, No. 335, Piscatory to Greek Minister of Foreign Affairs, Athenes, Fevrier 12, 1844.

79.   Kofas, *Politics in Greece,* 17.

80.   Hansard's Debates, 3rd series, LXXXII, 1280.

81.   British and Foreign State Papers, 1854-1855, XLV, 556-59.

82.   *Ibid.,* 566-68.

83.   Bower and Bolitho, *Otho,* 138-40.

84.   Hansard's Debates, 3rd series, LXXXIII, 1389-90.

85.   A. Y. E. 1847, 8/1, No. 33, Palmerston to Lyons, Foreign Office, April 6, 1847.

86.   A. Y. E. 1846, 8/1, (unnumbered) Kolettes, Athenes, Avril 18/ 30, 1846.

87.   Leconte, *Etude Economique,* 222.

88.   A. Y. E. 1846, 8/1, (unnumbered) Lyons to Kolettes, Athens, March 21, 1846.

89.   A. Y. E. 1846, 8/1 (unnumbered) Synedriasis Boules (Chamber of Deputies Session), Athens, October 8, 1846.

90.   E. About, *La Grece Contemporaine* (Athens, no date), 214.

91.   A. Y. E. 1847, 8/1, No. 316, Colettis aux Persiany et Lyons, Athenes, Janvier, 19/31, 1847.

92.   Hansard's Debates, 3rd series, XCII, 30.

93.   *Ibid.,* 313-23.

94.   Levandis, *Greek Foreign Debt,* 48.

95.   A.Y.E. 1847, 8/1, No. 33, Palmerston to Lyons, Foreign Office, April 6, 1847.

96.   A.Y.E. 1847, 8/1, No. 572, Otho, Athens, February 17, 1847.

97.   Hansard's Debates, 3rd series, XCII, 32.

98.   Levandis, *Greek Foreign Debt,* 48.

99.   A.Y.E. 1847, 8/1, No. 3150, Lyons to Coletti, Athens, July 8, 1847.

100. A.Y.E. 1847, 8/1, No. 1665, Eynard á Coletti, Mai 3, 1847.

101. A.Y.E. 1847, 8/1, No. 2238, Coletti é Eynard, Athenes, Juillet 8/20, 1847.

102. A.Y.E. 1847, 8/1, No. 2450, Lyons to Coletti, Athens, July 17/29, 1847.

103. A.Y.E. 1847, 8/1, No. 316, Coletti a Ministre de l'Angleterre et a Ministre de la Russie, Athenes, Janvier 19/31, 1847.

104. A.Y.E. 1847, 8/1, No. 1983, Lyons to Coletti, Athens, June 21, 1847.

105. A.Y.E. 1847, 8/1, No. 2449, Lyons to Coletti, Athens, July 30, 1847.

106. A.Y.E. 1847, 8/1, No. 3138, Lyons to Coletti, Athens, August 5, 1847.

107. *Ibid.*

108. Kofas, *Politics in Greece,* 16-21.

109. A.Y.E. 1847, 8/1, No. 2849, Lyons to Coletti, Athens, September 5, 1847.

110. A.Y.E. 1868, 8/1, (unnumbered) Etude sur l'emprunt contracte en 1832 par la Grece, avec la guarantie de la France, de la Grande Bretagne et de la Russie.

111. Kofas, *Politics in Greece,* 25.

112. For details on the administration from 1847 to 1853 see Aspreas, *Modern Greece,* I, 212-14, 219-20, also see Kordatos, *Modern Greece,* III, 441-85, and Kofas, *Politics in Greece,* 22-42.

113. For details on Kitsos Tzavellas, see Skandames, *Kingdom of Otho,* 678-94.

114. A.Y.E. 1847, 8/1, No. 3105, Lyons to Glarakis, Athens, September 21, 1847.

115. A.Y.E. 1847, 8/1, No. 3375, Lyons to Glarakis, Athens, October 10, 1847.

116. *Ibid.*

117. *Ibid.*

118. A.Y.E. 1847, 8/1, No. 3830, Lyons to Glarakis, Athens, November 22, 1847.

119. A.Y.E. 1847, 8/1, No. 4323, Lyons to Glarakis, Athens, January 8, 1848.

120. A.Y.E. 1847, 8/1, (unnumbered) Glarakis a Lyons, Athenes, Janvier 19/31, 1848.

121. A.Y.E. 1847, 8/1, No. 467, Lyons to Glarakis, Athens, January 31, 1848.

122. A.Y.E. 1848, 8/1, No. 302, Glarakis aux les charges d'affaires de la France et de la Russie, Athenes, Fevrier 11, 1848.

123. *Ibid.*

124. A.Y.E. 1848, 8/1, No. 565, Ministry of Finance to Glarakis, Athens, February 19, 1848.

125. A.Y.E. 1848, 8/1, No. 712, Lyons to Glarakis, Athens, March 9, 1848.

126. A.Y.E. 1848, 8/1, No. 759, Lyons to Glarakis, Athens, March 14, 1848.

127. A.Y.E. 1848, 8/1, Persiany a Glarakis, Athenes, Fevrier 6, 1848, also see A.Y.E. 1848, 8/1, (unnumbered) Thouvennel a Glarakis (no date).

128. For details on the revolts of 1848 see Vournas, *History,* 299-377, also see Kordatos, *Modern Greece,* III, 486-544.

129. Skandames, *Kingdom of Otho,* 694-726.

130. Thomaidou, *History of Otho,* 339-40.

131. Driault, *Histoire Diplomatique,* II, 321-22.

132. Dragoumes, *Recollections,* II, 134-35.

133. A.Y.E. 1848, 8/1, No. 1167, Lyons to Mansolas, Athens, April 12, 1848.

134. A.Y.E. 1848, 8/1, No. 3813, Lyons to Colokotronis, Athens, October 7, 1848.

135. Petropoulos, *Kingdom of Greece,* 321.

136. A.Y.E. 1848, 8/2, (unnumbered) Perglos a Colokotronis, Athenes, Decembre 16, 1848.

137. A.Y.E. 1848, 8/2, (unnumbered) Colokotronis a Perglos, Athenes, Decembre 14, 1848.

138. For more complete details concerning the British subjects' financial demands see British and Foreign State Papers, 1849-1850, XXXIX, 410-83, also see Thomaidou, *History of Otho,* 348-65.

139. Kofas, *Politics in Greece,* 28.

140. British and Foreign State Papers, 1849-1850, XXXIX, 485-600.

141. *Ibid.,* 601-883, also see Driault, *Histoire Diplomatique,* 341-61.

142. Kofas, *Politics in Greece,* 37-8.

143. There were many contributing elements to the Russophile tendencies of Greeks. In general the most important were Anglo-Greek antagonisms since 1837, the religious conflict in the Holy Places which involved the Catholics and Greek Orthodox supporters, and the Russian anti-Turkish foreign policy which enjoyed wide support in Greece. Kofas, *Politics in Greece,* 22-42.

144. For details concerning the Greek involvement in the Holy Places see Evagelides, *History of Otho,* 506-14, Fotiades, *The Exile,* 168-78, Kordatos, *Modern Greece,* III, 568-75, 594-98, and Kyriakides, *History,* I, 609-28.

145. Kofas, *Politics in Greece,* 39-42.

146. A. Y. E. 1852, 8/1, No. 741, Mavrokordatos a Paicos, Paris, Janvier 24, 1852.

147. *Ibid.*

148. A. Y. E. 1852, 8/1, No. 1703, Ministry of Finance to Ministry of Foreign Affairs, Athens, April 3, 1852.

149. *Ibid.*

150. A. Y. E. 1852, 8/2, No. 812, Perglos a Paicos, Athenes, Fevrier 2, 2852.

151. *Ibid.*

152. About, *Grece,* 214.

153. James Johnston Auchmuty, *Sir Thomas Wyse, 1791-1862* (London, 1939). This biography of Wyse examines the Minister's role in Greek politics from 1849 to 1862. The author of the biography has a highly favorable opinion about Wyse as a diplomat.

154. F.O. 32/205, No. 10, Wyse to Russell, Athens, February 3, 1853.

155. F.O. 32/205, No. 12, *Confidential,* Wyse to Russell, Athens, February 12, 1853.

156. Domna Donta, *E Ellas kai ai Dynameis kata ton Krimaikon Polemon* (Greece and the Powers During the Crimean War) (Thessalonike, 1973), 20, 66.

157. *Ibid.,* 67.

158. F.O. 32/314, No. 139, Wyse to Clarendon, Athens, October 27, 1853.

159. *Ibid.*

160. A. Y. E. 1854, 8/1, (unnumbered) Provelgios, Athens, February 11, 1854.

161. Donta, *Greece and the Powers,* 67.

162. F.O. 32/314, No. 139, *Confidential,* Wyse to Clarendon, Athens, October 27, 1853.

163. *Ibid.*

164. *Ibid.*

165. Donta, *Greece and the Powers,* 70.

166. F.O. 32/314, No. 139, *Confidential,* Wyse and Clarendon, Athens, October 27, 1853.

167. A. Y. E. 1853, 8/3, No. 7767, Paicos aux Tricoupis, Mavrokordato, et Zographos, Athenes, Novembre 27/Decembre 9, 1853, see also F.O. 32/314, (unnumbered) Paicos a Tricoupis, Athenes, Novembre 27/Decembre 9, 1853.

168. Donta, *Greece and the Powers,* 69.

169. A. Y. E. 1853, 8/3, No. 117, Trikoupis to Paicos, London, December 13/25, 1853, see also A. Y. E. 1853, 8/1, No. 7983, Wyse to Paicos, Athens, December 15, 1853.

170. F.O. 32/314, (unnumbered) Wyse to Paicos, Athens, January 5, 1853, also see A. Y. E. 1853, 8/3, No. 8473, Wyse to Paicos, Athens, January 5, 1853.

171. *Ibid.*

172. Donta, *Greece and the Powers,* 69.

173. For details on the causes of the Greek-Turkish hostilities of 1853-1854 *ibid.*, 25-26, Kofas, *Politics in Greece,* 42-63, and D. G. Koutroumbas, *E Epanastasis tou 1854 kai ai en Thessalia, Idia Epicheireseis* (The Revolution of 1854 and the Thessaly Undertaking) (Athens, 1976), 23-39.

174. A. Y. E. 1854, 8/1, No. 1718, Fourth-Rouen a Paicos, Athenes, Mars 9, 1854.

175. A. Y. E. 1854, 8/1, No. 1847, Wyse a Paicos, Athenes, Mars 27, 1854.

176. A. Y. E. 1854, 8/1, No. 1925, Wyse to Paicos, Athens, April 4, 1854.

177. A. Y. E. 1854, 8/1, No. 2248, Provelgios to Paicos, Athens, April 5, 1854.

178. A. Y. E. 1854, 8/1, No. 1841, Paicos aux Wyse et Forth-Rouen, Athenes, Mars 26/Avril 7, 1854, see also F.O. 32/314, (unnumbered) Paicos a Wyse, Athenes, Mars 26/Avril 7, 1854.

179. F.O. 32/314, (unnumbered) Wyse a Paicos, Athenes, Avril 11, 1854.

180. F.O. 32/208, (unnumbered) Wyse to Clarendon, Athens, 1854.

181. Kofas, *Politics in Greece*, 51-57.

182. F.O. 32/217, Circular, Wyse, May 30, 1854.

183. The Kriezes administration was dominated by Russophile politicians although there were a few Francophiles in the Cabinet. The entire administration with the exception of Spyridon Pelikas, Minister of Justice, supported Otho's irredentist policy. For more on this issue see Donta, *Greece and the Powers*, 15.

184. A. Y. E. 1854, 8/1, No. 3480, Mavrokordatos to Ministry of Finance, Athens, August 1854.

185. A. Y. E. 1854, 8/1, No. 5105, Mavrokordatos aux Forth-Rouen, Persiany et Wyse, Athenes, Septembre 10/22, 1854.

186. A. Y. E. 1854, 8/1, No. 5400, Persiany a Mavrokordato, Athenes, Septembre 11, 1854.

187. A. Y. E. 1854, 8/1, No. 5429, Forth-Rouen a Mavrokordato, Athenes, Septembre 28, 1854.

188. A. Y. E. 1854, 8/1, Extract, Drouen de Lhuys a Forth-Rouen, Paris, Octobre 9, 1854.

189. A. Y. E. 1854, 8/1, No. 190, Clarendon to Wyse Foreign Office, October 9, 1854.

190. A. Y. E. 1854, 8/1, No. 6091, Wyse to Mavrokordatos, Athens, October 28, 1854.

Notes to Chapter Three

1. Levandis, *Greek Foreign Debt*, 32.

2. British and Foreign State Papers, 1834-1835, XXIII, 961-65, and 1837-1838, XXVI, 126.

3. Sideris, *Agricultural Policy*, 31.

4. S. I. Tzivanopoulos, *Katastasis tes Ellados epi Othonos kai Prosdokiai Aftis ypo ten Aftou Megaliotera Georgiou A, Vasilea Ellinon* (The Condition of Greece under Otho and Her Expectations under His Majesty George I, King of the Greeks) (Athens, 1864), 33.

5. Sideris, *Agricultural Policy*, 30.

6. For details on the deplorable state of Greek agriculture during the early years of Otho's reign see Kordatos, *Modern Greece*, III, 11-20, Sideris, *Agricultural Policy*, 30-45, and Kyriakides, *History*, I, 26-27.

7. Leconte, *Etude Economique*, 307, and About, *Grece*, 93.

8. *Ibid.*, 99-100, see also Appendix B.

9. G. Zevgos, *Syntome Melete Neoellenikes Istorias* (A Short Study of Modern Greek History) (Athens, no date), II, 18.

10. *Ibid.*, 18.

11. A. Y. E. 1856, 8/1, No. 6912, Ministry of Finance to Ministry of Foreign Affairs, Athens, September 28, 1856.

12. Lignades, *Greek State*, 75-76.

13. Kostas Vergopoulos, *To Agrotiko Zetema sten Ellada* (The Agricultural Question in Greece) (Athens, 1975), 108, and Sideris, *Agricultural Policy*, 52.

14. See Appendix B.

15. Kofas, *Politics in Greece*, 115.

16. F.O. 32/244, No. 192, Wyse to Clarendon, Athens, August 12, 1856.

17. F.O. 32/314, No. 67, Clarendon to Wyse, Foreign Office, September 12, 1856.

18. *Ibid.*

19. A. Y. E. 1856, 8/1, No. 6668, Mercier a Ragabes, Athenes, Septembre 18, 1856.

20. F.O. 32/245, Wyse to Ragabes, Athens, September 25, 1856, also see A. Y. E. 1856, 8/1, No. 6554, Wyse to Ragabes, Athens, September 25, 1856.

21. F.O. 32/245, No. 221, Wyse to Clarendon, Athens, September 24, 1856.

22. A. Y. E. 1856, 8/1, No. 6912, Ministry of Finance to Ministry of Foreign Affairs, Athens, September 28, 1856.

23. *Ibid.*

24. F.O. 32/245, No. 230, *Confidential,* Wyse to Clarendon, Athens, October 7, 1856.

25. F.O. 32/314, *Memorandum,* Wyse to Clarendon, Athens, October 1856.

26. A. Y. E. 1856, 8/1, (unnumbered) Ragabe a Wyse, Athenes, Septembre 28, 1856.

27. *Ibid.*

28. A. Y. E. 1856, 8/1, No. 7158, Wyse to Ragabe, Athens, October 14, 1856.

29. A. Y. E. 1856, 8/1, (unnumbered) Ragabe a Wyse, Athenes, Octobre 6/18, 1856.

30. One of the most valuable informants to the British and French Legations at Athens was General Kalergis, an old enemy of King Otho. For more details see F.O. 32/245, No. 230, Wyse to Clarendon, Athens, October 7, 1856.

31. F.O. 32/245, (unnumbered) Wyse to Clarendon, Athens, October 27, 1856.

32. For details on the Financial Commission see Chapter IV.

33. A. Y. E. 1857, 8/1, Minister of Finance to Minister of Foreign Affairs, Athens, May 14, 1857.

34. F.O. 32/281, No. 63, Wyse to Malmesbury, Athens, June 17, 1858.

35. F.O. 32/283, (unnumbered) Wyse, Ozeroff, Montherot, Athens, May 12/24, 1859.

36. F.O. 32/282, (unnumbered) Wyse to Malmesbury, Athens, May 5, 1859.

37. F.O. 32/314, No. 31, Wyse to Russell, Athens, February 20, 1862.

38. F.O. 32/314, (unnumbered) Merlin to Wyse, Athens, February 22, 1862.

39. A. Y. E. 1862, a.a.k./A, (unnumbered) Wyse to Coundouriotes, Athens, February 25, 1862.

40. F.O. 32/314, (unnumbered) Eliot to Heliopoulos, Athens, July 2, 1862.

41. F.O. 32/314, No. 335, Napier to Russell, St. Petersburg, July 5, 1862, also see F.O. 32/314, No. 39, Eliot to Russell, Athens, September 28, 1862.

42. F.O. 32/357, (unnumbered) Deligiannes, Foreign Minister, Athens, January 2/14, 1864.

43. F.O. 32/488, Treasury 301, Foreign Office, January 6, 1879.

Notes to Chapter Four

1. Kofas, *Politics in Greece,* 116-17.

2. Skandames, *Kingdom of Otho,* 735-39.

3. F.O. 32/231, (unnumbered), *Confidential,* Wyse to Clarendon, Athens, September 29, 1855.

4. Kofas, *Politics in Greece,* 115-18.

5. F.O. 32/240, No. 70, Wyse to Clarendon, Athens, March 19, 1856.

6. A. Y. E. 1856, 8/1, No. 45, Emprunt, Grece, Mars 1, 1856.

7. A. Y. E. 1856, 8/1, No. 79, *Confidential,* Phocion Roques a Ragabe, Paris, Mars 30/Avril 11, 1856.

8. F.O. 32/240, No. 80, Wyse to Clarendon, Athens, April 12, 1856.

9. F.O. 32/242, No. 114, Wyse to Clarendon, Athens, June 18, 1856.

10. *Ibid.*

11. For German support of Otho at the Paris Peace Conference see Kofas, *Politics in Greece,* 115.

12. F.O. 32/242, No. 144, Wyse to Clarendon, Athens, June 18, 1856.

13. *Ibid.*

14. About, *Grece,* 122-23, also see Appendix A.

15. See Appendix A.

16. Kofas, *Politics in Greece,* 134-35.

17. F.O. 32/243, No. 162, Wyse to Clarendon, Athens, July 12, 1856.

18. *Ibid.*

19. A. Y. E. 1856, 8/1, No. 118, *Confidential,* Ragabes to Trikoupis, Athens, July 31/August 12, 1856.

20. *Ibid*

21. A. Y. E. 1856, 8/1, No. 127, *Confidential,* Trikoupis to Ragabes, London, August 12/24, 1856.

22. *Ibid.*

23. A. Y. E. 1856, 8/1, No. 125, *Confidential,* Trikoupis to Ragabes, London, August 10/22, 1856. Also A. Y. E. 1856, 8/1, No. 118, *Confidential,* Ragabes to Trikoupis, Athens, July 31/August 12, 1856.

24. A. Y. E. 1856, 8/1, No. 6032, Ministry of Finance to Ministry of Foreign Affairs, Athens, August 28, 1856.

25. A. Y. E. 1856, 8/1, (unnumbered) *Copy,* Ragabes to Trikoupis, Athens, (no date).

26. A.Y.E. 1858, 8/1, No. 140, *Confidential,* Trikoupis to Ragabes, London, September 10/22, 1856.

27. A.Y.E. 1856, 8/1, No. 134, *Confidential,* Ragabe aux Trikoupi et Roque, Athenes, Septembre 19/Octobre 1, 1856.

28. F.O. 32/280, (unnumbered) Trikoupi a Clarendon, Londres, Septembre 13/25, 1856.

29. *Ibid.*

30. A.Y.E. 1856, 8/1, No. 174, *Confidential,* Trikoupis to Ragabes, London, November 9/21, 1856.

31. F.O. 32/280, No. 333, *Confidential,* Wyse to Clarendon, Athens, October 21, 1856.

32. *Ibid.*

33. F.O. 32/280, No. 115, Wyse to Clarendon, Athens, October 28, 1856.

34. *Ibid.*

35. F.O. 32/246, No. 251, Wyse to Clarendon, Athens, November 4, 1856.

36. F.O. 32/280, No. 1378, Clarendon to Cowley, Foreign Office, November 18, 1856.

37. F.O. 32/280, (unnumbered) Cowley to Clarendon, Paris, November 14, 1856.

38. *Ibid.*

39. *Ibid.*

40. Kofas, *Politics in Greece,* 115-18.

41. F.O. 32/280, (unnumbered) Creptowitch to Clarendon, Londres, Novembre 17/29, 1856.

42. F.O. 32/280, No. 370, British Ambassy at St. Petersburg to Clarendon, St. Petersburg, November 28, 1856.

43. F.O. 32/280, No. 105, Clarendon to Wyse, Foreign Office, December 12, 1856.

44. For complete details on French, Russian and German diplomatic pressure on Britain in 1856 against the instalation of a Commission of unrestricted authority see A.Y.E. 1856, 8/1, (unnumbered) Perilepsis ton Ousioudeteron Energion Ypotheseos Daneiou apo ton Februario 1856.

45. A.Y.E. 1857, 8/1, No. 20, *Confidential,* Roque a Ragabe, Paris, Janvier 2/14, 1857.

46. A.Y.E. 1857, 8/1, (unnumbered) Soutzos a Ragabe, St. Petersburg, Janvier 2/14, 1857.

47. A.Y.E. 1857, 8/1, No. 20, *Confidentiel,* Roque a Ragabe, Paris, Janvier 2/14, 1857.

48. A.Y.E. 1857, 8/1, (unnumbered) Soutzos a Ragabe, St. Petersburg, Janvier 10/22, 1857.

49. A.Y.E. 1857, 8/1, No. 1, *Confidential,* Trikoupis to Ragabes, London, January 4/16, 1857.

50. A.Y.E. 1857, 8/1, No. 4, *Confidential,* Trikoupis to Ragabes, London, January 11/23, 1857.

51. F.O. 32/280, (unnumbered) Wyse to Clarendon, Athens, January 24, 1857.

52. A.Y.E. 1857, 8/1, No. 7, *Confidential,* Roque a Ragabe, Paris, Janvier 12/24, 1857.

53. A.Y.E. 1856, 8/1, No. 35, Walewski a Mercier, Paris, December 6, 1856, also A.Y.E. 1856, 8/1, No. 105, Clarendon to Wyse, Foreign Office, December 12, 1856.

54. A.Y.E. 1857, 8/1, No. 12, *Confidential,* Roque a Ragabe, Paris, Janvier 18/30, 1857.

55. A.Y.E. 1857, 8/1, No. 11, Trikoupis to Ragabes, London, February 1/13, 1857.

56. A.Y.E. 1857, 8/1, (unnumbered) Wyse to Ragabe, Athens, February 19, 1857.

57. A.Y.E. 1857, 95/2, No. 13, Trikoupis to Ragabe, London, February 4/16, 1857.

58. F.O. 32/280, (unnumbered) Wyse, Mercier, Persiany, Athenes, Fevrier 18, 1857.

59. *Ibid.*

60. F.O. 32/280, No. 11, Wyse to Clarendon, Athens, February 24, 1857.

61. F.O. 32/252, No. 35, Wyse to Clarendon, Athens, March 3, 1857.

62. F.O. 32/280, (unnumbered) Wyse to Clarendon, Athens, March 10, 1857.

63. Donald C. Blaisdell, *European Financial Control in the Ottoman Empire* (New YOrk, 1966), 28, 30. For the Ploeuc appointment to the Commission see A.Y.E. 1857, 8/1, No. 7, Walewski a Mercier, Paris, Fevrier 14, 1857.

64. F.O. 32/280, (unnumbered) Wyse to Clarendon, Athens, March 10, 1857.

65. A.Y.E. 1857, 8/1, No. 32, *Confidential,* Trikoupis to Ragabes, London, March 8/20, 1857.

66. A.Y.E. 1857, 8/1, (numbered) Expose de l'Etat Financier de la Grece emance du Ministere des Affaires Etrangeres.

67. *Ibid.*

68. A. Mansolas, *Politeiographikai Plerophoriai peri Ellados* (Politiographical Information Concerning Greece) (Athens, 1867), 199, Basile Digenis, *Quelques Notes Statistiques sur la Grece* (Marseille, 1877), 41-42, About, *Grece,* 127, and *Le Moniteur,* vol. 281, October 14, 1833.

69. About, *Grece,* 170.

70. Digenis, *Statistiques sur la Grece,* 21.

71. A.Y.E. 1857, 95/2, (unnumbered) Wyse to Ragabe, Athens, April 11, 1857.

72. A.Y.E. 1857, 95/2, No. 3255, Wyse to Ragabe, Athens, May 19, 1857.

73. A.Y.E. 1857, 95/2, No. 3441, Ministry of Finance to Ministry of Foreign Affairs, Athens, May 14, 1857.

74. A.Y.E. 1857, 95/2, (unnumbered) Wyse to Ragabe, Athens, May 28, 1857.

75. *Ibid.*

76. F.O. 32/280, (unnumbered) W. Campbell-Manley to ragabe, Athens, June 30, 1857.

77. On 2 March 1857 Koumoundouros, the Greek Minister of Finance, submitted to the Commission copies of the 1857 Budget. He explained that he could not provide the 1845 Budget, however, which Wyse wanted because no copies were made of it and only the Chamber of Deputies Reocrd would have it. See A.Y.E. 1857, 31/1, No. 1449, Koumoundouros to Ragabe, Athens, March 2, 1857.

78. A.Y.E. 1857, 95/2, (unnumbered) Strickland to Campbell-Manley, A.Y.E. 1857, 95/2, (unnumbered) Campbell-Manley to Ragabe, Athens, September 8, 1857.

79. F.O. 32/280, (unnumbered) Ragabe to Manley, Athenes, Septembre 19/Octobre 1, 1857.

80. A.Y.E. 1857, 95/2, No. 6717, Ozeroff a Ragabe, Athenes, Septembre 26, 1857, A.Y.E. 1857, 95/2, No. 7305, Ozeroff a Ragabe, Athenes, Octobre 22, 1857.

81.   F.O. 32/280, No. 144, Wyse to Clarendon, Athens, December 3, 1857.

82.   A.Y.E. 1857, 95/2, No. 1199, Soutsos a Ragabe, St. Petersburg, Decembre 10/22, 1857.

83.   A.Y.E. 1857, 95/2, No. 1201, Soutsos a Ragabe, St. Petersburg, Decembre 11/23, 1857.

84.   F.O. 32/280, No. 144, Wyse to Clarendon, Athens, December 3, 1857.

85.   F.O. 32/281, No. 8, Wyse to Clarendon, Athens, January 14, 1858.

86.   A.Y.E. 1858, 95/2, No. 897, Koumoundouros to Ragabe, Athens, February 8, 1858.

87.   A.Y.E. 1858, 95/2, (unnumbered) Ragabe a Wyse, Athenes, Fevrier 9/21, 1858.

88.   A.Y.E. 1858, 95/2, No. 839, Wyse to Ragabe, Athens, February 18, 1858.

89.   F.O. 32/281, No. 38, Wyse to Clarendon, Athens, February 24, 1858.

90.   F.O. 32/281, No. 38, Wyse to Clarendon, Athens, February 24, 1858.

91.   F.O. 32/281, No. 2, Wyse to Clarendon, Athens, March 18, 1858.

92.   F.O. 32/281, No. 13, Wyse to Clarendon, Athens, April 1, 1858.

93.   A.Y.E. 1858, 8/1, No. 2132, Ragabe a Roque, Athenes, Mars 19/31, 1858.

94.   F.O. 32/281, No. 13, Wyse to Clarendon, Athens, April 1, 1858.

95.   F.O. 32/281, No. 21, Wyse to Malesbury, Athens, April 15, 1858.

96.   *Ibid.*

97.   *Ibid.*

98.   *Ibid.*

99.   F.O. 32/281, No. 21, Wyse to Malmesbury, Athens, April 15, 1858.

100.   F.O. 32/281, No. 31, Wyse to Malesbury, Athens, April 29, 1858.

101.   *Ibid.*

102.   For a portrait of Charilaos Trikoupis' early career see Demetrios

Pournaras, *Charilaos Trikoupis* (Athens, 1976), I, 44-51.

103. A.Y.E. 1858, 95/2, No. 69, Trikoupis to Ragabe, London, May 15/27, 1858.

104. A.Y.E. 1858, 95/2, (unnumbered) Malmesbury to Trikoupi, Foreign Office, May 18, 1858.

105. A.Y.E. 1858, 95/2, (unnumbered) Trikoupi a Malmesbury, Londres, Mai 12/24, 1858.

106. *Ibid.*

107. A.Y.E. 1858, 95/2, No. 3150, Wyse to Ragabe, Athens, May 7, 1858, also F.O. 32/281, No. 40, Wyse to Malesbury, Athens, May 6, 1858.

108. A.Y.E. 1858, 95/2, No. 3736, Koumoundouros to Ragabe, Athens, May 15, 1858.

Extraordinary and Supplementary Credits

Ministry of Finance	1856-58	1,592,021 drachmas
Ministry of Justice	1856-57	104,000 drachmas
Ministry of Foreign Affairs	1856-57	118,028 drachmas
Ministry of Worship	1857-58	163,500 drachmas
Ministry of Military	1856-58	884,578 drachmas
Ministry of Interior	1856-58	2,456,543 drachmas
Ministry of Navy	1856-58	1,352,302 drachmas

109. A.Y.E. 1858, 95/2, No. 3944, Koumoundouros to Ministry of Foreign Affairs, Athens, May 22, 1858, also see A.Y.E. 1858, 95/2, No. 4395, Wyse to Ragabe, Athens, June 18, 1858.

110. F.O. 32/281, No. 86, Wyse to Malesbury, Athens, August 3, 1858.

111. F.O. 32/281, No. 109, Wyse to Malesbury, Athens, September 9, 1858.

112. A.Y.E. 1858, 95/2, No. 5946, Koumoundouros to Ragabe, Athens, July 18, 1858.

113. A.Y.E. 1858, 95/2, No. 5946, Koumoundouros a Wyse, Athenes, Juillet 31/Auout 12, 1858.

114. A.Y.E. 1858, 95/2, No. 6976, Ragabe a Wyse, Athenes, Novembre 13/25, 1858.

115. F.O. 32/281, No. 121, *Confidential*, Wyse to Malesbury, October 4, 1858.

116. *Ibid.*

117. *Ibid.*

118. A.Y.E. 1858, 95/2, No. 9219, Wyse to Ragabe, Athens, November 23, 1858, F.O. 32/282, (unnumbered) Protocole de 30 Seance de la Commission Financier, Wyse, Montherot, Ozeroff, Athenes, Decembre 24, 1858.

119. F.O. 32/282, No. 171, Wyse to Malmesbury, Athens, December 27, 1858.

120. A.Y.E. 1858, 95/2, No. 16224, Ministry of the Interior to Ministry of Foreign Affairs, Athens, (no date).

121. *Ibid.*

122. A.Y.E. 1858, 95/2, (unnumbered) Ministry of Finance to Thomas Wyse, Athens, (no date).

123. F.O. 32/282, No. 5, Wyse to Malmesbury, Athens, January 20, 1859.

124. F.O. 32/282, No. 12, Wyse to Malmesbury, Athens, February 10, 1859.

125. A.Y.E. 1859, 95/2, No. 755, Wyse to Ragabe, Athens, February 11, 1859, also see F.O. 32/282, (unnumbered) Wyse to Ragabe, Athens, February 11, 1859.

126. F.O. 32/282, (unnumbered) Wyse to Malmesbury, Athens, March 17, 1859.

127. A.Y.E. 1858, 95/2, (unnumbered) Ministry of Finance to Thomas Wyse, Athens, (no date), and F.O. 32/282, (unnumbered) Protocole of the 32nd Sitting of the Financial Commission, Wyse, Ozeroff and Montherot, Athens, (no date).

128. Mansolas, *Greece,* 178-79.

129. F.O. 32/282, (unnumbered) Wyse to Malmesbury, Athens, March 24, 1859.

130. F.O. 32/282, (unnumbered) Wyse to Malmesbury, Athens, May 12, 1858.

131. F.O. 32/282, (unnumbered) Wyse to Malmesbury, Athens, May 19, 1859.

132. *Ibid.*

133. F.O. 32/282, (unnumbered) Wyse to Malmesbury, Athens, May 26, 1859.

134. *Ibid.*

135. F.O. 32/282, (unnumbered) Memorandum, Wyse, Athens, May 26, 1859.

136. *Ibid.*

137. *Ibid.*

138. *Ibid.*

139. F.O. 32/282, (unnumbered) Wyse, Ozeroff, Montherot, Athens, May 12/24, 1859.

140. *Ibid.*

141. F.O. 32/282, No. 69, Wyse to Malmesbury, Athens, May 26, 1859.

142. F.O. 32/282, (unnumbered) Wyse, Ozeroff, Montherot, Athens, May 12/24, 1859.

143. A.Y.E. 1859, 8/1, No. 90, *Confidentiel,* Roque a Ragabe, Paris, Mai 23/Juin 4, 1859.

144. *Ibid.*

145. *Ibid.*

146. A.Y.E. 1859, 8/1, No. 95, *Confidentiel,* Roques a Ragabe, Paris, Mai 30/Juin 11, 1859.

147. F.O. 32/282, (unnumbered) Wyse to Russell, Athens, July 21, 1859.

148. A.Y.E. 1859, 8/1, No. 110, *Confidential,* Ragabes to Roques, Trikoupis, Zographos, Athens, August 27/September 8, 1859.

149. *Ibid.*

150. F.O. 32/282, No. 36, Wyse to Russell, Athens, September 2, 1859.

151. F.O. 32/282, No. 45, Wyse to Russell, Athens, October 21, 1859.

152. F.O. 32/282, (unnumbered) Ozeroff a Coundouriotes, Athenes, Octobre 9/21, 1859.

153. A.Y.E. 1859, 8/1, (unnumbered) Wyse to Koundouriotes, Athens, October 21, 1859.

154. F.O. 32/282, (unnumbered) Royal Address to the Chamber of Deputies, Athens, October 29, 1859.

155. F.O. 32/282, No. 52, Wyse to Russell, Athens, November 8, 1859.

156. A.Y.E. 1859, 8/1, No. 131, *Confidential,* Trikoupis to Koundouriotes, London, November 7/19, 1859.

157. A.Y.E. 1859, 8/1, No. 132, *Confidential,* Trikoupis to Koundouriotes, London, November 12/24, 1859.

158. A.Y.E. 1860, 8/1, No. 19, *Confidential,* Trikoupis to Zaimes, London, January 28/February 9, 1860.

159. *Ibid.*

160. F.O. 32/284, No. 24, Cornwallis to Russell, Athens, June 21, 1860.

161. A.Y.E. 1860, 8/1, Nos. 4268, 4269 & 4270, Coundouriotis aux Ministres du Roi a Paris, Londres et St. Petersburg, Athenes, Juin 9/21, 1860.

162. *Ibid.*

163. F.O. 32/283, (unnumbered) Coundouriotis a Trikoupis, Athenes, Juin 9/21, 1860.

164. A.Y.E. 1860, 8/1, Nos. 4268, 4269 & 4270, Coundouriotis aux Ministres du Roi a Paris, Londres et St. Petersburd, Athenes, Juin 9/21, 1860.

165. *Ibid.*

166. *Ibid.*

167. A.Y.E. 1860, 8/1, Nos. 2161, 2162 & 2170, Koundouriotes to Greek Embassies at St. Petersburg, London and Paris, Athens, June 9/21, 1860.

168. F.O. 32/283, (unnumbered) Cornwallis to Russell, Athens, June 27, 1860.

169. A.Y.E. 1860, 8/1, No. 99, Trikoupis to Koundouriotes, London, July 7/19, 1860.

170. A.Y.E. 1860, 8/1, No. 51, *Confidential,* Soutzos to Koundouriotes, St. Petersburg, July 15, 1860.

171. F.O. 32/283, (unnumbered) Coundouriotes a Cornwallis, Athenes, Juin 9/21, 1860.

172. F.O. 32/283, No. 275, Treasury Chambers to Foreign Office, London, October 18, 1860.

173. A.Y.E. 1861, 8/1, No. 66, Soutzos to Zaimes, St. Petersburg, March 19, 1861.

174. A.Y.E. 1861, 8/1, (unnumbered) Ozeroff a Coundouriotis, Athenes, Juillet 15/27, 1861.

175. F.O. 32/314, No. 259, Napier to Russell, St. Petersburg, August 21, 1861.

176. A.Y.E. 1861, 8/1, No. 90, *Confidential,* Trikoupis to Koundouriotes, London, July 28/August 9, 1861.

177. *Ibid.*

178. A.Y.E. 1861, 8/1, No. 92, *Confidential,* Trikoupis to Koundouriotes, London, August 3/15, 1861.

179. *Ibid.*

180. Kofas, *Politics in Greece,* 133.

181. F.O. 32/314, No. 259, Napier to Russell, St. Petersburg, August 21, 1861.

182. *Ibid.*

183. F.O. 32/314, No. 265, Napier to Russell, St. Petersburg, August 24, 1861.

184. F.O. 32/314, No. 279, Napier to Russell, St. Petersburg, August 27, 1861.

185. *Ibid.*

186. F.O. 32/314, No. 285, Napier to Russell, St. Petersburg, August 31, 1861.

187. A.Y.E. 1861, 8/1, No. 230, *Confidentiel,* Soutzos a Coundouriotis, St. Petersburg, Septembre 21, 1861.

188. F.O. 32/314, No. 119, Wyse to Russell, Athens, September 5, 1861.

189. *Ibid.*

190. F.O. 32/314, No. 128, Wyse to Russell, Athens, September 25, 1861.

191. F.O. 32/314, No. 135, Wyse to Russell, Athens, October 16, 1861.

192. *Ibid.*

193. F.O. 32/314, (unnumbered) Coundouriotis a Wyse, Athenes, Octobre 7/19, 1861, also see A.Y.E. 1861, 8/1, No. 6698, Coundouriotis a Wyse, Athenes, Octobre 7/19, 1861.

194. A.Y.E. 1861, 8/1, No. 6811, Quai d'Orsay, Paris, Octobre 23, 1861, also see A.Y.E. 1861, 8/1, Russell to Trikoupis, Foreign Office, October 16, 1861.

195. F.O. 32/314, No. 52, Palmerston to Wyse, Foreign Office, October 23, 1861.

196. F.O. 32/314, No. 31, Wyse to Russell, Athens, February 20, 1862.

197. F.O. 32/314, No. 63, Eliot to Russell, Athens, June 30, 1862.

198. *Ibid.*

199. A.Y.E. 1862, a.a.k./A, (unnumbered) Wyse to Koundouriotes, Athens, February 25, 1862.

200. F.O. 32/314, No. 63, Eliot to Russell, Athens, June 30, 1862.

201. F.O. 32/314, (unnumbered) Eliot to Heliopoulos, Athens, July 2, 1862.

202. A.Y.E. 1862, a.a.k./A, (unnumbered) Eliot to Heliopoulos, Athens, July 2, 1862.

203. F.O. 32/314, No. 335, Napier to Russell, St. Petersburg, July 5, 1862.

204. For details on the 1862 revolts at Nauplia see the diplomatic correspondence between the Greek Foreign Ministry and the Greek Embassy at London. A.Y.E. 1862, a.a.k./A, No. 873, Ministry of Foreign Affairs to Trikoupis, Athens, February 10/22, 1862, A.Y.E. 1862, a.a.a./A, No. 1148, Ministry of Foreign Affairs to Trikoupis, Athens, February 24/March 8, 1862, A.Y.E. 1862, a.a.k./A, No. 1475, Ministry of Foreign Affairs to Trikoupis, Athens, March 10/22, 1862, A.Y.E. 1862, a.a.k./A, (unnumbered) Ministry of Foreign Affairs to Trikoupis, Athens, March 22/April 3, 1862.

205. A.Y.E. 1862, a.a.k./A, No. 2129, Ministry of Foreign Affairs to Trikoupis, Athens, April 10/22, 1862.

206. A.Y.E. 1862, a.a.k./A, (unnumbered) Keliopoulos a Eliot, Athenes, Juin 19/31, 1862.

207. A.Y.E. 1862, a.a.k./A, No. 2651 & 3959, Heliopoulos to Trikoupis, Athens, June 28/July 10, 1862.

208. F.O. 32/314, No. 39, Eliot to Russell, Athens, September 28, 1862.

209. A.J.P. Taylor, *The Struggle for Mastery in Europe, 1848-1918* (Oxford, 1971), 126-32.

210. For details on Otho's exile see Fotiades, *The Exile,* 361-416, Vournas, *History,* 409-12, Aspreas, *Modern Greece,* I, 257-61, Kyriakides, *History,* II, 177-89.

211. F.O. 32/357, (unnumbered) F. Peel, Foreign Office, February 4, 1864.

Notes to Conclusion

1. F.O. 32/487, (unnumbered) *Confidential,* Memorendum, Foreign Office, January 6, 1871.

Notes to Appendices A and B

1. Kofas, *Politics in Greece,* 134-35.
2. A.Y.E. 1857, 95/2, No. 3002, Ministry of Finance to Ministry of Foreign Affairs, Athens, april 30, 1857.
3. *Ibid.*
4. A.Y.E. 1857, 95/2, (unnumbered) Wyse to Ragabes, Athens, June 3, 1857.
5. A.Y.E. 1857, 95/2, No. 2342, Wyse to Ragabes, Athens, April 15, 1857.
6. A.Y.E. 1857, 95/2, No. 3002, Ministry of Finance to Ministry of Foreign Affairs, Athens, April 30, 1857.
7. A.Y.E. 1857, 95/2, (unnumbered) Wyse to Ragabes, Athens, June 3, 1857.
8. *Ibid.*
9. A.Y.E. 1857, 95/2, No. 201, Mercier a Ragabe, Athenes, Janvier 24, 1857.
10. A.Y.E. 1857, 95/2, (unnumbered) Roques a Walewski, Paris, Mars 2/14, 1857.
11. A.Y.E. 1857, 95/2, No. 4526, Ministry of Finance to Ministry of Foreign Affaires, Athens, June 15, 1857.
12. A.Y.E. 1857, 95/2, (unnumbered) Ragabe a W.L. Manley, Athenes, Juillet 2, 1857.
13. A.Y.E. 1858, 95/2, No. 5946, Ministry of Finance, Athens, July 18, 1858.
14. *Kofas, Politics in Greece,* 28-29.
15. Anastasopoulos, *Greek Industry,* I, 101.
16. Mansolas, *Greece,* 51.
17. *Ibid.* ,56.

BIBLIOGRAPHY

ARCHIVES

1. The Archives of the Greek Ministry of Foreign Affairs. Athens.

1834	8/2	Daneion Bavarias (Bavarian Loan)
1844	8/1	Gallikon Daneion (French Loan)
1846	8/1	Peri Daneiou 60 Ekkatommyrion Fragon (Concerning the 60 Million Francs Loan)
1847	8/1	Peri Daneiou 60 Ekkatommyrion Drachmon (Concerning the 60 Million Drachmas Loan)
1848	8/1	Peri Daneiou 60 Ekkatommyrion Drachmon (Concerning the 60 Million Drachmas Loan)
1852	8/2	Bavarikon Daneion (Bavarian Loan)
1852	8/1	Peri Ellenikon Daneion (Concerning Greek Loans)
1853	8/1	Peri Daneion (Concerning Loan)
1853	8/3	Peri Daneiou 5 Ekkatommyriou Drachmon (Concerning a 5 Million Drachmas Loan)
1854	8/1	Peri Ellenikou Daneiou 60 Ekkatommyrion Drachmon (Concerning the Greek Loan of 60 Million Drachmas)
1854	8/3	Peri Daneiou 5 Ekkatommyrion Drachmon (Concerning the 5 Million Drachmas Loan)
1856	8/1	Peri Daneion (Concerning Loans)
1857	8/1	Peri Exameneias Tokon (Concerning the Six Month Interest)
1857	37/1	Apologismoi Esodon (Revenue Statements)
1857	95/2	Ypourgeion Oikonomikon (Ministry of Finance)
1858	8/1	Peri Ellenikou Daneiou (Concerning the Greek Loan)
1858	95/2	Ypourgeion Oikonomikon (Ministry of Finance)
1859	8/1	Peri Ellenikou Daneiou (Concerning the Greek Loan)

171

1859   95/2 Ypourgeion Oikonomikon (Ministry of Finance)
1860   8/1 Daneia (Loans)
1861   8/1, 2, 3 Peri Dieuthynseos Daneion (Cerning the Management
             of Loans)
1862   aak/A Allelographia Presbeias Londinou (Correspondence with
             the Embassy in London)

2. Public Record Office, London.
    Foreign Office Papers, vols. F.O. 32/205, 208, 217, 240, 242, 243,
    244, 245, 246, 252, 280, 281, 282, 283, 284, 314, 357, 487, 488

PUBLISHED SOURCES

I.   Printed Documents
     British and Foreign State Papers:
     Vols. XIV (1826-27), XXIII (1834-35), XXIV (1836-37), XXVI
     (1837-38), XXIX (1840-41), XLV (1854-55)
     Hansard's Parliamentary Debates, 3rd Series:
     Vols. 35 (1836, 69 (1843), 71 (1843), 82 (1845), 83 (1846) 92 (1847)

II. Memoirs, Biographies and Contemporary Accounts

     About, E. *La Grece Contemporaine.* Translated by A. Spelios, *E Ella-
         da tou Othonos (E Synchrone Ellada, 1854).* Athens: Tolides
         Bros., (no date).
     Bower, L. and Bolitho, G. *Otho I: King of Greece a Biography.* Lon-
         don: 1939.
     Digenis, Basile. *Quelques Notes Statistiques sur la Grece.* Marseille:
         Barlatier-Feissat, 1877.
     Dragoumes, N. *Listorikai Anamneseis* (Historical Recollections), 3rd
         ed., 2 vols. Athens: Stochaste, 1925.
     Evagelides, T. E. *Istoria tou Othonos Vasileos tes Ellados, 1832-1862*
         (History of Otho King of Greece, 1832-1862). Athens: Aristides
         G. Galanos, 1893.
     Fotiades, D. *Othonas: E Exosis* (Otho: The Exile). Athens: Dorikos,
         1975.
         . *Othonas: E Monarchia* (Otho: The Monarchy). Athens: Kypsele,
         1963.

Jarvis, George. *His Journal and Related Documents.* G. G. Arnakis, ed. Thessalonike: Institute for Balkan Studies, 1965.

Johnson, Douglas. *Guizot: Aspects of French History, 1787-1874.* Toronto: Routledge and Kegan Paul, 1963.

Kaldis, William P. *John Kapodistrias and the Modern Greek State.* Madison: University of Wisconsin, 1963.

Kolokotrones, Theodore. *Memoirs from the Greek War of Independence, 1821-1833.* Translated by G. Tertzetis. Chicago: Argonaut Press, 1969.

Koundouriotous Archeia, ed. A. Lignos. 5 vols. Pireaus; 1920-27.

Leconte, Casimir. *Etude Economique de la Grece.* Paris: 1847.

Mansolas, A. *Politeiographikai Plerophoriai peri Ellados* (Politiographical Information Concerning Greece). Athens: 1867.

Makrygiannes, G. *Makrygianne Apomnemoneumata* (Makrygianne Memoirs). Athens: Tolides, 1972.

Pournaras, Demitrios. *Charilaos Trikoupis.* 2 vols. Athens: Eleutheros, 1976.

The Greek Loans of 1824 & 1825. London: P. S. King, 1873.

Thomaidou, A. *Istoria Othonos* (History of Otho). Athens: Kosti Chairopoulos.

Tzivanopoulos, S. I. *Katastasis tes Ellados epi Othonos kai Prosdokiai Aftis ypo ten Aftou Megaliotera Georgiou A. Vasilea Ellinon* (The Condition of Greece under Otho and Her Expectations under His Majesty George I, King of the Greeks). Athens: K. N. B. Nake, 1864.

Woodhouse, C. M. *Capodistria: The Founder of Greek Independence.* London: Oxford University Press, 1973.

III. Monographs and General Accounts

Anastasopoulos, G. *Istoria tes Ellenikes Viomechanias, 1840-1940* (History of Greek Industry, 1840-1940). 2 vols. Athens: 1947.

Anderson, M. S. *The Eastern Question, 1774-1923.* New York: MacMillan, 1968.

Andreades, A. M. *Erga* (Works). 3 vols. Athens: 1938-1940.

Aspreas, G. *Politike Istoria tes Neoteras Ellados* (Political History of Modern Greece). 3 vols. Athens: Chrisima Biblia, no date.

Auchmuty, James J. *Sir Thomas Wyse, 1791-1862.* London: 1939.

Blaisdell, Donald C. *European Financial Control in the Ottoman Empire.*
New York: A.M.S. Press, 1966.

Charitakes, G. *E Ellenike Viomechania* (Greek Industry). Athens: Estia,
1927.

Clayton, G.D. *Britain and the Eastern Question: Messolonghi to Gallipoli.* London: University of London Press, 1971.

Clogg, Richard, ed. *The Movement for Greek Independence, 1770-1821.*
London: Harper Row, Inc., 1976.

————, ed. *The Struggle for Greek Independence.* London: Archon
Books, 1973.

Crawley, C.W. *The Question of Greek Independence.* Cambridge: 1930.

Dakin, Douglas. *The Greek Struggle for Independence, 1821-1833.*
Berkley: University of California press, 1973.

Daskalakes, G.D. *Ellenike Syntagmatike Istoria, 1821-1935* (Greek Constitutional History, 1821-1935). Athens: 1951.

Diamantouros, N.P. et al., eds. *Hellenism and the First War of Liberation,
1821-1830.* Thessalonike: Institute for Balkan Studies, 1976.

Donta, Domna. *E Ellas kai ai Dynameis kata ton Krimaikon Polemon*
(Greece and the Powers During the Crimean War). Thessalonike:
Institute for Balkan Studies, 1973.

Driault, Edouard and Lheritier, Michel. *Histoire Diplomatique de la
Grece de 1821 a nos jours.* 5 vols. Paris: Les Presses Universitaires
de France, 1925-1926.

Evelpides, Chrysos. *E Georgia tes Ellados* (Greek Agriculture). Athens:
1944.

Finlay, George. *History of the Greek Revolution and the Reign of King
Otho.* London: Zeno, 1971.

Howarth, David. *The Greek Adventure.* New York: Atheneu, 1976.

Jelavich, Barbara. *Russia and the Greek Revolution of 1843.* Munich:
1966.

————. *Russia and Greece During the Regency of King Otho, 1832-
1835.* Thessalonike: Institute for Balkan Studies, 1962.

Jenks, Leland H. *The Migration of British Capital to 1875.* London:
Thomas Nelson, Ltd., 1927.

Kissinger, Henry. *A World Restored.* Boston: Houghton Miffin Co.,
1973.

Kofas, Jon V. *International and Domestic Politics in Greece During the Crimean War.* New York: East European Monographs, Columbia University Press, 1980.

Kokkinos, D. *E Ellenike Epanastasis* (The Greek Revolution). 6 vols. Athens: 1931-35.

Kordatos, Giannes. *E Koinonike Semasia tes Ellenikes Epanastaseos tou 1821* (The Social Significance of the Greek Revolution of 1821). Athens: 1946.

————. *Istoria tes Neoteres Elladas* (History of Modern Greece). 5 vols. Athens: 1957-58.

Koutroumbas, D.G. *E Epanastasis tou 1854 kai ai en Thessalia, Idia, Epichereseis* (The Revolution of 1854 and the Thessaly Undertaking). Athens: 1976.

Kyriakides, E. *Istoria tou Synchronou Ellinismou apo tes Idryseos tou Vasileiou tes Hellados, 1832-1892* (History of Contemporary Greeks from the Founding of the Kingdom of Greece, 1832-1892). 2 vols. Athens: B.N. Gregoriades, 1972.

Laskaris, L. Th. *Diplomatike Istoria tes Ellados, 1821-1914* (Diplomatic History of Greece, 1821-1914). Athens: 1947.

Levandis, J.A. *The Greek Foreign Debt and the Great Powers, 1821-1898.* New York: Columbia University, 1944.

Lignades, Anastasion D. *E Xenike Exartesis kata ten Diadromen tou Neoellinikou Kratous, 1821-1945* (The Foreign Dependence During the Course of the Modern Greek State, 1821-1945). Athens: 1975.

————. *To Proton Daneion tes Anexartesias* (The First Loan of Independence). Athens: 1970.

Marriot, J.A.R. *The Eastern Question.* Oxford: Clarendon Press, 1969.

Markezines, S.B. *Politike Istoria tes Neoteras Ellados* (Political History of Modern Greece). 4 vols. Athens: Papyros, 1966.

Mexas, B. *Oi Philikoi.* Athens, 1947.

Moskof, Kostes. *E Ethnike kai Koinonike Syneidese sten Ellada, 1830-1909* (The National and Social Conscience in Greece, 1830-1909 (The National and Social Conscience in Greece, 1830-1909). Athens, 1974.

Petropoulos, J.A. *Politics and Statecraft in the Kingdom of Greece, 1833-1843.* Princeton, N.J.: Princeton University Press, 1968.

Sideris, A. E. *Georgike Politike tes Ellados* (The Agricultural Policy of Greece). Athens: 1933.

Skandames, A. *Selides Politikes Istorias kai Kritikes, E Triakontaetia tes Vasileias tou Othonos, 1832-1862* (Pages of Political History and Critique, the Thirty-year Kingdom of Otho, 1832-1862). Athens: 1961.

St. Clair, William. *That Greece Might Still be Free.* London: Oxford University Press, 1972.

Strupp, K., ed. *La Situation International de la Grece, 1821-1917; Recueil de documents choisis et edites avec une introduction historique et dogmatique.* Zurich: 1918.

Svolos, Alexander. *Ta Ellenika Syntagmata, 1822-1952* (The Greek Constitutions, 1822-1952). Athens: Stochastes, 1972.

Taylor, A.J.P. *The Struggle for Mastery in Europe, 1848-1918.* London, Oxford, New York: Oxford University Press: 1971.

Vergopoulos, Kostas. *To Agrotiko Zetema sten Ellada* (The Agricultural Question in Greece). Athens: Exantas, 1975.

Vournas, Tasos. *Armatoloi kai Klephtes.* Athens: 1958.

————. Istoria tes Neoteres Elladas (History of Modern Greece). Athens: Tolides Bros., 1974.

Webster, C.F. *The Foreign Policy of Palmerston, 1830-1841.* 2 vols. London: 1951.

Woodhouse, C.M. *The Philhellenes.* Madison: Farleigh Dickinson University Press, 1971.

Zakynthinos, D.A. *The Making of Modern Greece.* Translated by K.R. Johnston. Oxford: Basil Blackwell, 1976.

Zevgos, G. *Sentome Melete Neoellenikes Istorias* (A Short Study of Modern Greek History). Athens: P. Nasiote, (no date).

Zographos, Demetrios L. *Istoria Ellenikes Georgias, 1821-1833* (History of Greek Agriculture, 1821-1833). Athens: Eleutheros, 1923.

INDEX

EAST EUROPEAN MONOGRAPHS

The *East European Monographs* comprise scholarly books on the history and civilization of Eastern Europe. They are published by the *East European Quarterly* in the belief that these studies contribute substantially to the knowledge of the area and serve to stimulate scholarship and research.

Political Ideas and the Enlightenment in the Romanian Principalities, 1750-1831. By Vlad Georgescu. 1971.

America, Italy and the Birth of Yugoslavia, 1917-1919. By Dragan R. Zivjinovic. 1972.

Jewish Nobles and Geniuses in Modern Hungary. By William O. McCagg, Jr. 1972.

Mixail Soloxov in Yugoslavia: Reception and Literary Impact. By Robert F. Price. 1973.

The Historical and National Thought of Nicolae Iorga. By William O. Oldson. 1973.

Guide to Polish Libraries and Archives. By Richard C. Lewanski. 1974.

Vienna Broadcasts to Slovakia, 1938-1939: A Case Study in Subversion. By Henry Delfiner. 1974.

The 1917 Revolution in Latvia. By Andrew Ezergailis. 1974.

The Ukraine in the United Nations Organization: A Study in Soviet Foreign Policy. 1944-1950. By Konstantin Sawczuk. 1975.

The Bosnian Church: A New Interpretation. By John V. A. Fine, Jr., 1975.

Intellectual and Social Developments in the Habsburg Empire from Maria Theresa to World War I. Edited by Stanley B. Winters and Joseph Held. 1975.

Ljudevit Gaj and the Illyrian Movement. By Elinor Murray Despalatovic. 1975.

Tolerance and Movements of Religious Dissent in Eastern Europe. Edited by Bela K. Kiraly. 1975.

The Parish Republic: Hlinka's Slovak People's Party, 1939-1945. By Yeshayahu Jelinek. 1976.

The Russian Annexation of Bessarabia, 1774-1828. By George F. Jewsbury. 1976.

Modern Hungarian Historiography. By Steven Bela Vardy. 1976.

Values and Community in Multi-National Yugoslavia. By Gary K. Bertsch. 1976.

The Greek Socialist Movement and the First World War: The Road to Unity. By George B. Leon. 1976.

The Radical Left in the Hungarian Revolution of 1848. By Laszlo Deme. 1976.

The Catholic Church, Dissent and Nationality in Soviet Lithuania. By V. Stanley Vardys. 1978.

The Development of Parliamentary Government in Serbia. By Alex N. Dragnich. 1978.

Divide and Conquer: German Efforts to Conclude a Separate Peace, 1914-1918. By L. L. Farrar, Jr. 1978.

The Prague Slav Congress of 1848. By Lawrence D. Orton. 1978.

The Nobility and the Making of the Hussite Revolution. By John M. Klassen. 1978.

The Cultural Limits of Revolutionary Politics: Change and Continuity in Socialist Czechoslovakia. By David W. Paul. 1979.

On the Border of War and Peace: Polish Intelligence and Diplomacy in 1937-1939 and the Origins of the Ultra Secret. By Richard A. Woytak. 1979.

Bear and Foxes: The International Relations of the East European States 1965-1969. By Ronald Haly Linden. 1979.

Czechoslovakia: The Heritage of Ages Past. Edited by Ivan Volgyes and Hans Brisch. 1979.

Prima Minister Gyula Andrassy's Influence on Habsburg Foreign Policy. By Janos Decsy. 1979.

Citizens for the Fatherland: Education, Educators, and Pedagogical Ideals in Eighteenth Century Russia. By J. L. Black. 1979.

A History of the "Proletariat": The Emergence of Marxism in the Kingdom of Poland, 1870-1887. By Norman M. Naimark. 1979.

The Slovak Autonomy Movement, 1935-1939: A Study in Unrelenting Nationalism. By Dorothea H. El Mallakh. 1979.

Diplomat in Exile: Francis Pulszky's Political Activities in England, 1849-1860. By Thomas Kabdebo. 1979.

The German Struggle Against the Yugoslav Guerrillas in World War II: German Counter-Insurgency in Yugoslavia, 1941-1943. By Paul N. Hehn. 1979.

The Emergence of the Romanian National State. By Gerald J. Bobango. 1979.

Stewards of the Land: The American Farm School and Modern Greece. By Brenda L. Marder. 1979.

Roman Dmowski: Party, Tactics, Ideology, 1895-1907. By Alvin M. Fountain, II. 1980.

International and Domestic Politics in Greece During the Crimean War. By Jon V. Kofas. 1980.

Fires on the Mountain: The Macedonian Revolutionary Movement and the Kidnapping of Ellen Stone. By Laura Beth Sherman. 1980.

The Modernization of Agriculture: Rural Transformation in Hungary, 1848-1975. Edited by Joseph Held. 1980.

Britain and the War for Yugoslavia, 1940-1943. By Mark C. Wheeler. 1980.

The Turn to the Right: The Ideological Origins and Development of Ukrainian Nationalism, 1919-1929. By Alexander J. Motyl. 1980.

The Maple Leaf and the White Eagle: Canadian-Polish Relations, 1918-1978. By Aloysius Balawyder. 1980.

Antecedents of Revolution: Alexander I and the Polish Congress Kingdom, 1815-1825. By Frank W. Thackeray. 1980.

Blood Libel at Tiszaeszlar. By Andrew Handler. 1980.

Democratic Centralism in Romania: A Study of Local Communist Politics. By Daniel N. Nelson. 1980.

The Challenge of Communist Education: A Look at the German Democratic Republic. By Margrete Siebert Klein. 1980.

The Fortifications and Defense of Constantinople. By Byron C.P. Tsangadas. 1980.

Balkan Cultural Studies. By Stavro Skendi. 1980.

Studies in Ethnicity: The East European Experience in America. Edited by Charles A. Ward, Philip Shahshko, and Donald E. Pienkos. 1980.

The Logic of "Normalization:" The Soviet Intervention in Czechoslovakia and the Czechoslovak Response. By Fred Eidlin. 1980.

Red Cross. Black Eagle: A Biography of Albania's American School. By Joan Fultz Kontos. 1981.

Nationalism in Contemporary Europe. By Franjo Tudjman. 1981.

Great Power Rivalry at the Turkish Straits: The Montreux Conference and Convention of 1936. By Anthony R. DeLuca. 1981.

Islam Under the Double Eagle: The Muslims of Bosnia and Hercegovina, 1878-1914. By Robert J. Donia. 1981.

Five Eleventh Century Hungarian Kings: Their Policies and Their Relations with Rome. By Z.J. Kosztolnyik. 1981.

Prelude to Appeasement: East European Central Diplomacy in the Early 1930's. By Lisanne Radice. 1981.

The Soviet Regime in Czechoslovakia. By Zdenek Krystufek. 1981.

School Strikes in Prussian Poland, 1901-1907: The Struggle Over Bilingual Education. By John J. Kulczycki. 1981.

Romantic Nationalism and Liberalism: Joachim Lelewel and the Polish National Idea. By Joan S. Skurnowicz. 1981.

The "Thaw" In Bulgarian Literature. By Atanas Slavov. 1981.

The Political Thought of Thomas G. Masaryk. By roman Szporluk. 1981.

Prussian Poland in the German Empire, 1871-1900. By Richard Blanke. 1981.

The Mazepists: Ukrainian Separatism in the Early Eighteenth Century. By Orest Subtelny. 1981.

The Battle for the Marchlands: The Russo-Polish Campaign of 1920. By Adam Zamoyski. 1981.

Milovan Djilas: A Revolutionary as a Writer. By Dennis Reinhartz. 1981.

Hungary between Wilson and Lenin: The Hungarian Revolution of 1918-1919 and the Big Three. By Peter Pastor. 1976.

The Crises of France's East-Central European Diplomacy, 1933-1938. By Anthony J. Komjathy. 1976.

Polish Politics and National Reform, 1775-1788. By Daniel Stone. 1976.

The Habsburg Empire in World War I. Robert A. Kann, Bela K. Kiraly, and Paula S. Fichtner, eds. 1977.

The Slovenes and Yugoslavism, 1890-1914. By Carole Rogel. 1977.

German-Hungarian Relations and the Swabian Problem. By Thomas Spira. 1977.

The Metamorphosis of a Social Class in Hungary During the Reign of Young Franz Joseph. By Peter I. Hidas. 1977.

Tax Reform in Eighteenth Century Lombardy. By Daniel M. Klang. 1977.

Tradition versus Revolution: Russia and the Balkans in 1917. By Robert H. Johnston. 1977.

Winter into Spring: The Czechoslovak Press and the Reform Movement 1963-1968. By Frank L. Kaplan. 1977.

The Catholic Church and the Soviet Government, 1939-1949. By Dennis J. Dunn. 1977.

The Hungarian Labor Service System, 1939-1945. By Randolph L Braham. 1977.

Consciousness and History: Nationalist Critics of Greek Society 1897-1914. By Gerasimos Augustinos. 1977.

Emigration in Polish Social and Political Thought, 1870-1914. By Benjamin P. Murdzek. 1977.

Serbian Poetry and Milutin Bojic. By Mihailo Dordevic. 1977.

The Baranya Dispute: Diplomacy in the Vortex of Ideologies, 1918-1921. By Leslie C. Tihany. 1978.

The United States in Prague, 1945-1948. By Walter Ullmann. 1978.

Rush to the Alps: The Evolution of Vacationing in Switzerland. By Paul P. Bernard. 1978.

Transportation in Eastern Europe: Empirical Findings. By Bogdan Mieczkowski. 1978.

The Polish Underground State: A Guide to the Underground, 1939-1945. By Stefan Korbonski. 1978.

The Hungarian Revolution of 1956 in Retrospect. Edited by Bela K. Kiraly and Paul Jonas. 1978.

Boleslaw Limanowski (1835-1935): A Study in Socialism and Nationalism. By Kazimiera Janina Cottam. 1978.

The Lingering Shadow of Nazism: The Austrian Independent Party Movement Since 1945. By Max E. Riedlsperger. 1978.